Basic Bible Sermons on Spiritual Living

BASIC BIBLE SERMONS

ON

SPIRITUAL LIVING

Stephen B. McSwain

BROADMAN PRESS
NASHVILLE, TENNESSEE

Unless otherwise noted, all Scripture quotations are taken from the *New King James Version*. Copyright © 1979, 1980, 1982, Thomas Nelson, Inc., Publishers.

All Scripture quotations marked (RSV) are from the *Revised Standard Version of the Bible*, copyrighted 1946, 1952, © 1971, 1973.

All Scripture quotations marked (KJV) are from the *King James Version* of the Bible.

Library of Congress Cataloging-in-Publication Data

McSwain, Stephen B., 1955-
    Basic Bible sermons on spiritual living / Stephen B. McSwain.
        p.   cm. — (Basic Bible sermons series)
    ISBN 0-8054-2274-9 : $4.95
    1. Baptists—Sermons.   2. Sermons, American.   I. Title.
II. Series.
BX6333.M3875B37   1991
252'.061—dc20   91-10198
                                                              CIP

Other Books in the Basic Bible Sermons Series:

Basic Bible Sermons on the Cross, W. A. Criswell
Basic Bible Sermons on Easter, Chevis F. Horne
Basic Bible Sermons on John, Herschel H. Hobbs
Basic Bible Sermons on the Church, Ralph Smith
Basic Bible Sermons on Hope, David Farmer
Basic Bible Sermons on Philippians, J. B. Fowler, Jr.

Contents

1. Through Assurance 11
   (Romans 3:21-31)
2. Through Integrity 19
   (1 Peter 3:15; Romans 5:1-5)
3. Through Confidence 28
   (Romans 1:16; 1 Timothy 1:8-14)
4. Through Discipleship 36
   (Luke 14:25-33)
5. Through Mission 45
   (Jonah 1—4)
6. Through Triumph 53
   (2 Corinthians 2:5-16)
7. Through Stewardship 60
   (2 Corinthians 9:1-15)
8. Through Courage 68
   (1 Samuel 17; Philippians 4:13)
9. Through Worship 76
   (Mark 2:1-12)
10. Through Intimacy 84
    (Psalm 127)
11. Through Trust 92
    (Numbers 13:25-33; Matthew 6:25-34)
12. Through Security 100
    (2 Corinthians 5:1-10)
13. Through Perseverance 108
    (Hebrews 12:1-2)
14. Through Devotion 117
    (Psalm 46:10; Luke 10:38 to 11:13)
Notes 125

Preface

In Aristotelian philosophy, *energy* is the activity that transforms potentiality into actuality. In Pauline theology Christ is the *energy* by which our potentiality is transformed into actuality. In Ephesians 4:15-16, Paul writes, "Christ, from whom the whole body, joined and knit together by what every joint supplies, according to the effective working *[activity* or *energy]* by which every part does its share, causes growth of the body for the edifying of itself in love."

This book is about Christ and the energy He supplies every Christian to achieve her or his highest spiritual potential. The "whole body" (the church) depends upon "every part" (each Christian) achieving his/her spiritual potential for its effectiveness.

How? What is the key to maximizing your Christian potential? The key is found not in you alone but Christ in you. A church Father, Saint Augustine, once prayed, "Give what you command, and command what you will." God commands and demands much from those who would follow Him. What is wonderfully liberating, however, is that God supplies us with the qualities He expects from us.

What is it God expects of us? He expects faithfulness in all things, integrity both within and without, confidence in the face of difficulty, trust when it would be much easier to doubt, hope in the presence of despair, perseverance in our "toss-in-the-towel" society, and intimacy both with Him and each other. These expectations are the essentials for dynamic living. At times, however, it is a struggle to develop these essentials.

Do you have difficulty being faithful? Feeling confident? Having courage? Staying in the race? Do the essentials for dynamic living often escape you? Then, this book is for you. It is written to help you achieve your highest spiritual potential (which is what God expects) by reminding you of the means available to you (which is Christ in you). The indwelling presence of Christ energizes the spirit life of every Christian. You have within you the *energy* by which your potentiality is transformed into actuality. "Christ in you, the hope of glory" (Col. 1:27, KJV).

So, begin now energizing your spirit life through Christ who lives in you and provides to you the essentials for dynamic living.

1
Through Assurance

What Are Your Chances of Going to Heaven?

(ROMANS 3:21-31)

In a recent edition of *USA Weekend*, the findings of a poll conducted across America were published. The question raised was, "What are your chances of going to heaven?" Seventy-two percent of the U.S. citizens interviewed rated their chances of making it to heaven as good to excellent. One man from Illinois rated his chances of going to heaven at fifty-fifty. "The older I get, the more I think my chances will improve," the man said.

Another responded, "I don't think the entrance exam will be all that tough!"

And, one woman from Indiana said, "You have to be more than a nice person. But, I'm still in the running."[1]

Before explaining the question scripturally, a few observations are in order. To begin with, many of the respondents expressed the belief that going to heaven is a matter of chance. Are they right? Is it just a gamble like going to the races and hoping you've wagered on the right horse? Or, is going to heaven something more than a matter of chance?

In addition to this, many of those responding indicated an understanding of salvation based on human effort. For example, with regard to the matter of going to heaven, one person said, "You just have to be a good person." Is that all it takes? Just being a good person? Trying to live right and not breaking the Ten Commandments?

A third observation regards the Bible itself. What does the Bible say about one's chances of going to heaven? None of the respon-

dents seemed remotely aware of the scriptural requirements of going to heaven. Since it is from the Scriptures that we learn what little
we know about heaven, it would seem there should be a desire on
the part of people to know what the Bible says about the subject.
But, interestingly, many neither know the Scriptures nor display
much curiosity in settling the question once and for all from the
standpoint of the Bible.

What are your chances of going to heaven? I believe the question itself raises an existential anxiety in all of us. We want to know
even though we may treat the subject somewhat flippantly. I am
convinced that, until the question is settled in our own hearts and
minds, our anxiety will remain. Conversely, when we have answered the question scripturally, we will be free to celebrate life and
face death and eternity with fearless assurance.

In the event you've not guessed already, I'm convinced what
the Bible says about getting into heaven is right. Scripture is my
authority. If you do not share my conviction, read the next chapter. If
you do, it is my hope that the paragraphs which follow will help you
settle the question in your own mind and set you free to live life in
all its fullness.

Read Romans 3:21-31. It is the heart of the gospel, the good
news about Jesus Christ. The apostle Paul makes two basic points in
this passage with multiple illustrations drawn from his rich Hebrew
heritage.

The Human Problem

The first point he makes relates to our common human problem. "For all have sinned and fall short of the glory of God" (v. 23).
In the mind of Paul, all human beings (Jew, Gentile or otherwise)
have one basic problem. We are sinners. The Greek verb translated
sinned means to miss the mark. It is a word drawn from the athletic
world which relates to the idea of a marksman's arrow missing the
target. The expression *fall short* is a second athletically related phrase
which connotes the idea of a runner falling behind in a race.

What did Paul want to say to his readers by the employment of
these two ideas? Simply, humans are incredibly inept, even with all

our capabilities, at being morally and ethically righteous before God. The word *righteous* means to live in such a way as to be morally and ethically pleasing to God.

In recent years, the tendency has been to look upon people who are well-educated and culturally refined as outside the need of God's grace and forgiveness. We have no problem looking at those at the bottom of society's rung as in need of redemption. However, for those who through education and cultural development improve their social standing, we sometimes forget that in every person, "The heart is deceitful above all things, and desperately wicked" (Jer. 17:9, KJV). It makes no difference if that heart beats in the chest of a Harvard graduate or a Harlem beggar. Both persons are in need of God's grace and forgiveness. True righteousness is impossible apart from God's help.

Recently, a major newspaper reported that one of the nation's most eminent psychiatrists resigned his position at Harvard Medical School after admitting he had plagarized large sections of several articles he wrote in medical journals and textbooks.[2] When I first read the story, I wondered how a man of his intellectual prowess, educational accomplishment, and social grace could succumb to something like plagarism. But then, I remembered Paul's words that we all "fall short" and "miss the mark." We are all sinners. The human problem is the same for all humans, regardless.

Paul was writing about persons not unlike many today who thought they could be pleasing and acceptable to God by a meticulous obedience of all God's laws. The Bible makes clear that, in spite of our best intentions, we fall short of God's expectations and miss the mark of perfection. In short, we need help. Which of us would be so bold as to claim we've never made a mistake?

Once a minister was trying to make the point that we are all guilty and imperfect. After a series of rhetorical questions, he asked his congregation, "Is there any person here who would dare to claim you've never made a mistake—that you are perfect? If so, stand up!"

He scanned the congregation for any response, but of course, there was none. Just as he prepared to proceed with the message, however, one man sitting near the back stood to his feet.

Somewhat startled, the minister questioned him, "Sir, do you claim to be perfect?"

"Oh, no," retorted the man. "I just thought someone should stand on behalf of my wife's first husband!"

We laugh about that only because it is preposterous to think that any of us are in any way perfect. There are two options open to the person who wants to be acceptable to God. Either he can set out to live a life that will be so perfectly pleasing to God that he will be rewarded with eternal life, or he may decide that is hopeless and trust himself completely to God who is able to do for him what he cannot do for himself.[3]

The Divine Provision

This is where Paul makes his second point which relates to God's provision for our human problem. In verses 24-25, Paul describes what God has done for persons like us who fall short of His expectations. It all relates to what Jesus has accomplished for us on the cross. To help us understand, Paul used three illustrations. Each one provides a beautiful facet of truth in the diamond of God's provision of Jesus Christ.

Justified

The first illustration is drawn from the court of law and the important word *justified* (v. 24*a*, KJV). The active form of the verb means to pronounce righteous, put in the right, or acquit. It is a legal term and pictures a guilty person standing before a righteous judge awaiting his dreadful sentence. The verdict comes back however, "Not guilty." Humans are guilty. We fall short. Yet, when the expected verdict is guilty, God remarkably declares "not guilty" to those who trust in Jesus Christ.

Redemption

A second illustration is drawn from the slave market. The word is *redemption* (v. 24*b*, KJV). While the force of the metaphor may escape us who live in the modern world, it was familiar to people in

New Testament times. Slaves were brought to the marketplace where potential buyers gathered. The buyers would examine them and, if they so desired, would buy them by paying a lutron—a ransom price. Thus, a slave's liberation was purchased by a liberator.

Paul viewed all humans like slaves held captive by sin and incapable of delivering themselves. Christ is the liberator who purchases the freedom by paying the ransom price Himself. Enslaved by sin, people are set free by Christ.

Propitiation

The final illustration used by Paul to depict God's provision for the human predicament is that of the altar of sacrifice. The word is *propitiation* (v. 25, KJV). In biblical Greek, the verb form is a sacrificial term describing the annulment of sin. Some Scripture scholars feel a better word for translating this Greek word would be *expiation* or the means of forgiveness. As such, it would refer to the mercy seat described in Exodus 25. In ancient Hebrew practice, the high priest annually made atonement for the sins of Israel by taking a blood sacrifice into the holy of holies and sprinkling it on the mercy seat. Therefore, Paul was saying that the crucified Christ became for the world what the mercy seat was for the Israelites.[4] The death of Christ on the cross becomes the means by which we may experience the mercy, grace, and forgiveness of God.

In verse 27, Paul asks, "Where is boasting then?" (KJV) That's like asking "From where does one sense of confidence come with regard to one's eternal destiny?" Does it come from obedience to God's laws as the people of Paul's day might have argued? It would if people could fulfill the demands of the law without error, but such is impossible.

Does it come from trying to live a good life and hoping God will reward our feeble attempts as many in the *USA Weekend* survey seem to believe? It would if God expected us to be sincere people with good intentions.

Neither approach, however, is acceptable to God. There is only one way to be right with God and settle the question of our eternal destiny. It is the way of faith—faith in the Christ who has done for us what we are incapable of doing for ourselves. What does it mean to have faith in Jesus Christ?

Recently, a man who attends the church I serve was cutting firewood alone in the woods. As he was cutting down a huge tree, an unexpected and tragic event occurred. The tree rebounded off a limb nearby causing the base of the falling tree to swirl off its stump and land on his leg. He suffered a crushing blow to his right foot and ankle so severe that were it not for the leather boot he was wearing, his foot would have been severed at the ankle. Being a strong man, he sought to drag himself nearly a mile to the outskirts of the woods in spite of the difficulty and excruciating pain. It became increasingly apparent to him, however, he was not going to make it. At that point, he called for help. A farmer in a field nearby heard his pleas for help and came to assist him. Soon a rescue team in a helicopter flew him to a hospital where emergency surgery took place. Today, as I write these words, he is recovering with the hope that, not only will his foot be saved from amputation, he will walk again someday.

His experience serves as an example of the meaning of faith. Although he may have wanted to be able to get to the hospital on his own, the fact is he had no option but to admit it was an impossible task and trust himself to the rescuers who could do for him what he was incapable of doing for himself. That's what it means to have faith in Jesus. While we may want to entertain the illusion that our goodness merits the grace of God, the fact is our goodness is hardly good enough. To trust Jesus means that I admit there is no way to win God's favor by winsome self-effort, but by a grateful acceptance of His Divine assistance.

Having seen, then, what God has done for us in Jesus Christ, we face again the question of the survey. What are your chances of going to heaven? Three observations are in order; the conclusion of which I hope will help you settle the question in your own mind once and for all.

Not chance, but choice.—First, going to heaven is not a matter of chance, but choice. The choice is yours as well as mine. We may choose the way of self-effort and be destined to live a frustrated and defeated life. We may choose the way of chance and be destined to live in uncertainty and fearfulness. Or, we may choose God's way which is the way of faith in Jesus Christ and live, not only in this life, but in the life to come. The choice is there. The decision is yours. Jesus said,

> Enter by the narrow gate; for wide is the gate and broad is the way that leads to destruction, and there are many who go in by it [namely all those who through self-effort or self-justification try to improve their chances]. Because narrow is the gate and difficult is the way which leads to life, and there are few who find it (Matt. 7:13-14).

But, you may find it. God's way is right before you. The issue is, "Will you choose it?"

Not human achievement, but humble acceptance.—A second observation is that going to heaven is not a matter of human achievement, but humble acceptance. In the survey, a woman from Indiana said that to go to heaven "you have to be a good person." But, if going to heaven is a matter of human achievement, then we are competitors at best. I compete against you and you against me. Which one of us will win the race? The one, of course, who runs the best and fastest. The mere thought of it is depressing, if not demeaning. God will have no part of it. He is not in the business of setting people at odds with each other by making them competitors who compete for His grace. Yet, there are people who believe your eternal destiny is determined by deeds done here on earth. I heard about a person who said, "My greatest fear in life is that I will be standing behind Mother Teresa and I'll hear God say to her: 'You know, Mother Teresa, you should have done more.'" What an atrocious idea! It is not only scripturally incorrect, but it makes us all competitors trying to outdo each other and accomplish our own salvation. On the contrary, going to heaven is a matter of humble acceptance. Like the man with a fractured foot, we acknowledge our utter helplessness and humbly turn ourselves over to the One who can truly help us. Karl Barth once said that whenever we speak of our virtues and achievements we are mere competitors. When, however, we confess our sins, we are brothers and sisters.

Not a future concern, but a confession today.—A final observation is that going to heaven is not a matter of future concern, but confession today. The Bible says, "Now is the day of salvation" (2 Cor. 6:2, KJV). Far too many people go through life hoping, wishing, and wondering if they will make it to heaven. What freedom there is to live captive to fear? The issue may be settled today. Your wishes and hopes about heaven can be turned into realities.

How? By praying a prayer similar to the following:

> Lord, I know I am a sinner. I cannot save myself, and I'm tired of trying. From now on, I'm going to trust You to be my Savior and Lord and do in me and through me what I cannot do for myself. Thank You for giving Your life to me. Help me as I begin living my life for you. In Jesus' name, Amen.

If you have never prayed such a prayer, do so now. Then, find a local church in which you can begin living for Christ in and through that church. Do you know what will happen if you pray that prayer and trust your life and future to Jesus Christ? You'll settle the question of going to heaven once and for all and that assurance will energize your spiritual life.

2
Through Integrity

On Knowing "Why" You Are a Christian

(1 PETER 3:15; ROMANS 5:1-5)

"Why are you a Christian?" asked a young man while I was a second-year seminary student. I stumbled over his question because, the truth is, I had never given it much thought. Over the years I have come to believe it is one of the most formational questions of identity and, more importantly, integrity. Psychologists tell us it's important to know "who" we are. Ask a person today who he or she is, and you are likely to receive such responses as: "I'm a schoolteacher"; "I'm an assembly line worker"; "I'm a surgeon"; "I'm a pastor"; "I'm a housewife (house husband)"; or "I'm a seminary student."

While it is important to know *who* you are, I think it is more important to know *why* you are. Why are you a schoolteacher, factory worker, minister, doctor, or seminary student? And, equally as important, "Why are you a Christian?" Knowing *who* you are will give you a sense of identity. Knowing *why* you are, on the other hand, will clothe your identity with integrity. The word *integrity* comes from the Latin word *integritas* meaning the state or condition of being complete or whole. Integrity is knowing *why* you are *who* you are. It's important to be a Christian. That's the mark of identity for many of us. It is also important to know why you're a Christian. That's the mark of integrity which many of us need.

The apostle Peter instructed the Christians in Asia Minor, "And always be ready to give a defense to everyone who asks you a reason for the hope that is in you" (1 Pet. 3:15). The word *defense* translates a Greek word which is our word *apology*. Peter says, be ready to give [an apology] for the hope that is in you." Give an apology? Is Peter suggesting we apologize for our faith? Of course not! The word *apology* is a legal term. It means to develop a defense as an attorney might in a court of law. It means to give a reason or explanation as a parent might to an inquisitive child.

Over the years, I've given much thought to the question, and I believe it must be addressed before one's Christian identity will have any integrity about it. So, why am I a Christian? I've listed some reasons.

The Process of Becoming

I am who I am because, to a large extent, it is the natural result of my upbringing. I'm a preacher's kid. I grew up in the church. I have known nothing but the church all my life. My father tells me that, shortly after bringing me home from the hospital, he and mother dedicated me unto the Lord. They told me the stories of Christ and instructed me in the ways of Christ.

I can never remember a time that I did not love Jesus. Some of my earliest memories as a child are those of singing in Sunday School, "Jesus loves me! this I know, For the Bible tells me so." I spent so much of my childhood at church that it was as if the Sunday School rooms of the educational building were simply additions to the church parsonage. I'll never forget being caught by my father one Saturday as my brother and I went swimming in the church baptistry. To us, it was the church's private health spa.

At the age of seven, I made a profession of faith. The Sunday night I walked the church aisle is as vivid in my mind as the sun is bright in my eyes. What was my theological depth at the time of my conversion? Pretty elementary, but my spiritual experience was unforgettably significant. Whatever else may have happened that night, it's certain my spiritual pilgrimage began.

In *Glad Reunion*, John Claypool speaks of two types of conversion. One type he calls a "revolutionary" conversion, or the apostle Paul type (see Acts 9). The other he calls the "evolutionary" conversion, or the Timothy type (see 2 Tim. 1:5).[1] The latter describes my experience. I evolved into the experience of becoming a Christian.

My experience is hardly unique. I've watched with interest over the years this process of becoming Christian in the lives of many believers. In fact, I'm convinced this is the most common experience of salvation. In the church, we place an inordinate amount of interest in the dramatic conversion experience, leaving many evolutionary types wondering if their religious experience is as genuine. The church all too frequently applauds those who graphically testify to living a life filled with immoral behavior, plummenting to the depths of despair, meeting Christ in a spectacular encounter, and then rising to the heights of moral, spiritual, and often financial success. Such conversion experiences are not in question. However, I think it's time the church applauds those whose lives have been lived faithfully in the context of the Christian community. Such persons seldom paint pictures of what it's like to live in the "world" (that place some revolutionaries can paint vividly, and that place I wonder if some are sorry they ever left), but evolutionary types most often and, most certainly, stroke the canvas of human life with designs which leave the world a more beautiful place.

How is it with you? Does the description of my experience sound like yours? Change our names, occupations of our parents, the location of our community, and the rest of our stories sound similar. How do you feel about your religious heritage? I used to despise mine. I grew up in the era of the sixties and seventies. Sociologists observe it as a period of social change. They are wrong. The only thing that changed was the length of hair. Those of us who found it fashionable to be "hippie-types" and rebel against everything which appeared to be "institutional" are now the fashion-conscious "yuppie-types." We now embrace the things we once wagged our heads, disapprovingly, toward our parents for seeking.

It has been my observation over the years that the church is filled with many who, like me, are reared in the church, make a profession of faith early in life, reach the teenage years, and suddenly find themselves asking questions many Christian parents fear their children might ask: "Why should I have to go to church? Is Christianity true? Is there really a God?" Christian parents should not be too alarmed, however, when their children ask questions. These questions are different ways of asking, "Why am I a Christian?" They are questions which need to be asked. If they are not asked when the teenager becomes an adult, he or she may have a Christian identity, but there will be little or no integrity about it. Integrity is what identity needs. Why am I a Christian? I am a Christian because my heritage brought me to the place where the experience of God's grace was natural.

What the Christian Faith Offers Us

There's a second reason why I'm a Christian. I'm convinced the Christian faith is unparallelled in what it offers to the human family. According to the apostle Paul, the Christian faith offers us peace with God (Rom. 5:1). To be at peace with God is to be at peace with oneself. Not that the self is God, but the self cannot be truly itself apart from God.

Consider also, the Christian faith offers us "access by faith into this grace" (v. 2). What does that mean? It means that our faith in Christ grants us the ominous privilege of laying hold on God's grace and presence. He is in us. We are in Him. He surrounds, undergirds, and sustains us through all of life's experiences. We have His undivided attention. My own child may compete with all the other persons and things that clamor for my attention as his earthly father, but a child of God never has that problem with the Heavenly Father. He is nearer to us than the air we breathe.

Being Christian also offers us a new way of looking at life's troubles and tragedies. The apostle Paul put it, "And not only that, but we also glory in tribulations" (v. 13). "Glory in tribulations?" Exactly! How so? By recognizing that the difficulties of life provide us with an opportunity for growth. That's not to say that God is the author of trouble. But it is to say that, given the reality of a life filled with problems, accidents, and tragedies, God may use those experiences to help our faith deepen and develop.

In the parish I serve, there is a devoted Christian mother who gave birth some years ago to a Down syndrome child. I asked her one day what it was like giving birth and rearing her daughter Elaine.

"Well," she explained, "when Elaine was born, I'll never forget how everyone who came to see me, including the doctor, and cried, 'Oh what a terrible tragedy!' But, you know," she said, "somehow, I never saw the tragedy!" As she talked, I thought about Paul's words, "We also glory in tribulations."

Two poems sharply contrast what the world offers with what Christ offers us. William Ernest Henley wrote "Invictus."

> Out of the night that covers me,
>   Black as the Pit from pole to pole,
> I thank whatever gods may be
>   For my unconquerable soul.
>
> In the fell clutch of circumstance
>   I have not winced nor cried aloud.
> Under the bludgeonings of chance
>   My head is bloody, but unbowed.
>
> Beyond this place of wrath and tears
>   Looms but the Horror of the shade
> And yet the menace of the years
>   Finds, and shall find me, unafraid.
>
> It matters not how strait the gate,
>   How charged with punishments the scroll,
> I am the master of my fate,
>   I am the captain of my soul.

On the surface, these words are appealing. However, they are words of foolish bravery underscored by the fact that the man who wrote the poem took his own life in despair. Dorothea Day wrote a Christian response to "Invictus."

> Out of the light that dazzles me,
>   Bright as the sun from pole to pole
> I thank the God I know to be
>   For Christ—the Conqueror of my soul.
>
> Since His the sway of circumstance
>   I would not wince, nor cry aloud.
> Under the rule which men call chance,
>   My head, with joy, is humbly bowed.

Beyond this place of sin and tears,
    That life with Him—And His the aid
That, spite the menace of the years,
    Keeps, and will keep me, unafraid.

I have no fear though strait the gate:
    He cleared from punishment, the scroll.
Christ is the Master of my fate;
    Christ is the captain of my soul.

The Christian faith offers something unparalleled by this world and what it may pretend to offer us—peace with God, preeminence with God, and a new perspective toward trouble.

Christianity and the World Religions

Why am I a Christian? A third reason is found in the radical difference I've discovered between Christianity and many of the world religions. There is much Christians in the Western world could learn from the practitioners of the Eastern religions, if we were not closed-minded. There is also much we can teach those in other religious traditions. Namely, we could teach them the watershed difference that exists between Christianity and the religions of the world. For, in Christianity, we have the distinct privilege of knowing, intimately and personally, the God who is not "far from each one of us; for in Him we live and move and have our being" (Acts 17:27-28). Christ, who many search in hope of finding, is the God many worship in ignorance.

Using the heavenly constellations as an illustration of human understanding of God, someone has helpfully stated that those who practice the Eastern religions have a "starlight" understanding of God. Those who worship in monotheistic traditions (religions that believe in one God such as Islam and Judaism) have a "moonlight" understanding of God, while Christianity provides its adherents with "Son-light."[2] We know God most completely when we meet Him in Christ. Evangelistic zeal should find its impetus in the conviction that we have something to tell those who know something about God, just not enough.

There's a second watershed difference between Christianity and the other religions of the world. It's best described in a story I heard a professor tell in class several years ago. G. Earl Guinn was conducting a revival in a large downtown church in New Orleans. After the service, he met a young man whom he thought at first was a common drifter. After a few minutes conversation, Guinn learned he was a Ph.D. graduate of Columbia University.

On the day of his graduation, his wife filed for divorce, and his life fell apart. A few weeks later, he attempted to end his life. During his hospital stay, a group of women from a Baptist church visited him regularly and made him promise if he ever had those feelings of despair again to seek the help of a minister. That promise brought him to the church where Guinn was preaching. The two of them went to the pastor's study where they talked for several hours. He encouraged the troubled man, prayed with him, and sent him home.

Guinn shared with our class that, while they talked, the young man made an interesting observation. He said,

> Dr. Guinn, I've studied many of the religions of the world including Christianity. One thing impressed me, a thought from which I've never been able to escape. In all the religions of the world, the emphasis is always on man and what man must do, sacrificially, in order to appease and please the gods. The one exception I discovered, however, is in Christianity. In the Christian faith, the emphasis is always upon God and what He sacrifices on behalf of the human family.

A twinkle came to Guinn's eyes as he said to us, "You know something? He's exactly right! The major difference between Christianity and other world religions lies in the fact that Christ is God's sacrificial gift on behalf of the human family."

I thought to myself, *That's it! That's the difference between Christianity and all other religions of the world*. And, that's one of the significant reasons why I am a Christian.

A Different Kind of World

There's one final reason. As I have reflected on the ethical implications of Christianity, I've become convinced when the faith is modeled after its Founder, it can establish the kind of world in which we all want to live.

Jesus said, "Follow Me." That means to go where Jesus would go, do what Jesus would do, say what Jesus would say, think what Jesus would think, and feel what Jesus would feel. The problem with those of us in the Western church is that we have become all too casual about Christianity. A famous author once said that we don't know if Christianity can work. Only one man lived it the way it should be lived, and he died prematurely. The issue is not, however, "Can Christianity work?" We know it can. The real issue is, "Will it work?" That's a question which can be answered only in the heart of every believer.

What kind of world would this be if every Christian seriously took the call to be a true follower of Christ by seeking to know, before any word, act, or deed, "What would Jesus do if He were facing my circumstances?"

What I am saying is dramatically illustrated in the story of a little handicapped boy who sold candy in the lobby of a busy airport terminal. Every day his guardians brought him to the airport where he would sit on a stool behind a portable stand and sell candy to the passengers.

One morning, a man was in a hurry to catch a plane. Racing around a corner, he stumbled into the boy sending him in one direction, the stool in another, and the candy scattered everywhere. Rather than apologizing, the angry passenger shouted obscenities at the boy as he pulled himself up from the floor and hurried off to catch his plane.

There was another traveler who was following close behind. He, too, was in a hurry, but rather than stepping around the boy, he stopped, picked up the boy's stool, lifted the youngster back into position, and retrieved as much of the candy as he could. Reaching into his pocket, he handed the boy a five dollar bill along with a kind word, "Son, I hope this will help offset some of your loss today. God bless you, little fella!" Standing up, he headed toward his plane.

He was stopped, however, by the piercing shrill of the little boy's voice as he shouted at him, "Mister! Mister!" The man turned around and the boy called out loudly, "Mister, are you Jesus?"

Stunned by his question, the man walked back to the boy, knelt down in front of him, and said with a smile, "No, son, I'm not Jesus. But, I am one of His followers, and He has taught me to care for people just like you." And, with that, he disappeared into the crowd.

What the world can be is limited only by the Christian's imagination. What the world will be is limited only by the Christian's inclination.

Why are you a Christian? Only you can answer that question. But, if you will, your Christian identity will develop integrity. And, when you do develop integrity, this world of ours will be a more *integritas* place in which to live.

3
Through Confidence

*Raising Your Level
of Confidence*

(ROMANS 1:16; 1 TIMOTHY 1:8-14)

"I am not ashamed of the gospel," shouted the apostle Paul. He might not have been, but most of us are.

At school? At work? Or, the bridge party? The discussion turns to religion or the latest clergy scandal, and everyone speaks disdainfully about the church's hypocrisy. Don't you feel like a fool at times to admit you're a Christian these days?

Why is there little boldness these days about the Christian faith? While there may be many reasons for our feelings of timidity, one reason is the Bible itself. Many people today view the Bible as simply a collection of myths and fairy tales—clever to read but hardly acceptable to the scientific mind.

"You believe the Bible?" one man asked me as if surprised. "Why it's so antiquated and full of myths. How can you believe all that stuff you read?"

He has a point. The Bible is hard to believe, even harder to explain. Since the dawn of the Freudian era, we have come to think about the world in ways different from our ancestors. Herein, I believe, is one source of our embarrassment.

The Jewish rabbi Harold Kushner touches on it in a story he tells of a boy who was asked by his mother what he had learned in church school that day. The boy described the story of the Israelites' exodus from Egypt, but when he came to the dramatic portion about the crossing of the Red Sea, he edited the story saying, "Moses took out his walkie-talkie and called in the Israeli Air Force to bomb the Egyptians, while the others built a pontoon bridge to cross over the Red Sea."

Perplexed at his version of the story, the boy's mother asked, "Is that how they told you the story?"

He dropped his head and muttered, "Well no, Mom, but if I told you the story the way they told it to me, you'd never believe it!"[1]

That's our problem, isn't it? Whenever we read the Bible, we are suddenly thrust into a world which seems foreign to us. A world where seas part and folks trek across on dry ground; bushes burn but are not consumed; manna drops out of the sky to feed hungry people; folks walk on water; the blind are given their sight; quadriplegics are made to walk; and the dead are brought back to life. How do you explain that kind of world to a world accustomed to analyzing itself under a microscope?

My point? You can't explain it! The stories of our faith live on from generation to generation, not because skilled practitioners of religious truth perfect better ways of explaining the stories but because the stories themselves have a life of their own. They need no explanation. They need simply to be told. The more we seek to reduce the Christian narrative to a carefully categorized set of propositions, the greater our anxiety will be about the Bible and our faith. In short, the more we try to explain the Bible, the less confidence we have in the Bible.

It's time we let the Christian story speak for itself. Its story is our story. If our interest is in strengthening the believing person's confidence so he or she can say with the apostle Paul, "I am not ashamed of the gospel," we will come closer to accomplishing that objective, not by wrangling over whether the hare chews the cud (Lev. 11:6), but by affirming the truth of the Christian story. Need we be ashamed? Absolutely not!

I've listed a few reasons why we need not be ashamed of the Christian faith.

Promises

To begin with, we may be proud of the Christian faith because it does not disappoint.

We are a suspicious people. And, we have a right to be because we are bombarded on every front by promises which usually turn

out to be disappointments. Consider, for example, the average television advertisement. An announcer reminds aging women with
encroaching facial wrinkles that, if they will use a certain product,
they will likely live to be as old as Methuselah. Granted the adver-
tisers don't go quite that far, but they do promise a youthful appear-
ance for the duration of your life. Any thinking person, however,
knows that's not true.

We've been promised so much, and the return has been so little
that most of us feel a little like Spike who wrote Snoopy a letter in
one of the "Peanuts" episodes. "Dear Snoopy, I've just purchased a
magic cape from a door-to-door salesman who promises me that, if I
wear the cape, I will be instantly transported to a land of paradise.
So, by the time you get this letter, I'll be in paradise." Several frames
pass and in the final scene, Spike is standing right smack in the
middle of a desert surrounded by cactus plants. In the caption below, Spike is complaining, "Somehow, I think I've been had."

Spike's problem is our problem. We've been "had" too many
times. We are understandably suspicious. The unfortunate thing is
that it affects the way many of us look at the Christian faith. However, the Christian faith does not disappoint. It does produce what it
promises.

What does the Christian faith promise? It promises to put you
in a right relationship with God. A popular Christian song says that
people need the Lord. They do. When we come into the world,
we're OK. But then, something goes wrong. All of us fall subject to
the effects of what theologians call "original sin." What is original
sin? Frederick Buechner says that *original sin* means we all originate
out of a sinful world which taints us from the word go. We all tend to
make ourselves the center of the universe.[2] When we make ourselves the center of the universe, then we're lost to Him who is the
origin of the universe. That's what it means to be lost. In our lost-
ness, God comes to find us. Like a celestial "Hound of Heaven," He
pursues us until we find Him. That does not mean everyone will
find the Lord, however. Some will be like the fellow who woke up in
the middle of the night hungry. Opening the refrigerator door, he
stood there feeling hungry but not knowing what he was hungry for.

Those who do find the Lord and are found by Him, however, will discover their deepest hungers satisfied.

The second thing the Christian faith promises to do is to put you in a right relationship to others. The Christian church is an amazing institution, isn't it? Our critics say the church is responsible for much of the cruelty experienced in the world. Our history is undeniably imperfect. The amazing thing to me is that, with all our imperfections, neither I or anyone else would wish to live in this world without the church.

God has come in Christ to show us how to love and respect one another and to live free of a spirit of revenge toward those who have wronged us. Recently, I heard a story which illustrates the spirit of revenge. A fellow was driving down Hollywood Boulevard looking at the homes of movie stars. Passing by one attractive home, he saw a new Mercedes parked out front with a sign on it which read: "For Sale, $100." Stopping, he went to the door and inquired about the Mercedes. "Is it true you are selling it for $100?"

"That's what the sign says!" said the woman who answered the door.

Without hesitating he proceeded to purchase the car. When the transaction was complete he asked, "How is it that you can sell this new Mercedes for $100?"

Angrily she said, "Last week, my husband ran off with his secretary. He called this morning from Hawaii to tell me he had run out of money. He asked me to sell his car and send him the cash. So, that's what I'm doing!"

Now, that's revenge. Such behavior need not be your response to mistreatment. The Christian faith promises to empower you to release your feelings of resentment and positively seek reconciliation with those who have wronged you.

It promises to give us victory over our personal sins. All of us wrestle with a skeleton in our closet. Perhaps it's a bad habit, a loose tongue, a debilitating lust, or an insatiable greed. Christ has come to help us with our "sin" problem and empower us in dealing with our personal sins.

Margaret Slatterly worked for years in the slum sections of Chicago. One day she met Freddy who was paralyzed from his waist down. An operation would make it possible for Freddy to walk but the cost of hospitalization crushed all hopes. Margaret Slatterly made the boy's situation known to the nation and solicited the needed funds for the operation. After weeks of recovery from the surgery, the day came when Freddy was to try to take his first steps.

Freddy's parents said, "Margaret, if our son is able to walk, we want him to take his first steps toward you." With great effort, Freddy slowly stood up and managed to take a few awkward steps toward Margaret. In time, Freddy was able to walk and run as other children.

Years later as Margaret Slatterly was speaking to a group of persons, she said, "I wish I could tell you Freddy is now standing on those two legs and helping others as a surgeon or a minister. But, I cannot. Freddy is in a federal prison for committing a heinous crime against another human being." She ended her speech with the provocative statement, "I have long since learned that medical science can help a boy to walk, but only God can help him walk in the right direction."[3]

Promises, promises, promises. They are everywhere. The Christian faith really does deliver what it promises. It will help you know God's forgiveness, learn to be forgiving, and experience victory over sin.

Needs

There is a second reason why we need not be ashamed of the Christian faith. It fulfills our most basic human needs. Someone has said that all humans have three basic needs—to be noticed, nurtured, and needed.

A popular movie star was quoted as saying that all my life, I have wanted the whole world to know who I am, to love me, and to be affected by me. While she may not know it, she was saying, "I need to be noticed, nurtured, and needed." We all do. The Christian faith meets all these needs.

Carl Sandburg once said, "We all want to play Hamlet!" Perhaps he overstated the case, but it's true that we all want to be recognized. The cross of Jesus Christ is the single most poignant statement of our significance to God. When Jesus died on the cross it was as if God Himself were saying, "You're somebody special!"

Remember the nursery rhyme?

> Humpty Dumpty sat on a wall,
> Humpty Dumpty took a great fall;
> All the king's horses
> And all the king's men,
> Couldn't put Humpty Dumpty together again.

Who can put Humpty Dumpty back together again? A contemporary song, "Where do broken hearts go?" Where do they go? The Christian faith says, "Come to God through Jesus Christ!" I'm convinced one of the reasons that the poor, brokenhearted, and disenfranchised people came to Jesus with such openness and joy was because they felt He understood their condition and would help them put their lives together again.

Shakespeare had one of his characters say, "Life's . . . it is a tale/ Told by an idiot, full of sound and fury,/Signifying nothing." Is that true? Perhaps for some, but, the Christian faith gives rhyme and reason to our living. By living as Christ lived—sharing words of hope where there is hopelessness; ministering to lives broken by sin, suffering, and disease; and offering love to the loveless, faith to the faithless, and strength to the powerless—we may hold our heads high, confident there is purpose, meaning, and goodness in all of life lived after the fashion of Christ Himself. The Christian faith answers our need for significance, sympathy, and service.

Hope

There's a final reason why we can have confidence in the Christian faith. It provides us with a hope that will not die. The hope is expressed in two ways. First, we live with the hope for a better world. The theologian, Emil Brunner, once said that what oxygen is to the lungs, hope is to human life. Without hope, we die. With it, however, we live.

The voices of doom are everywhere. Surprisingly, they are even heard among those of us who should, of all people, be the most hopeful. It is as if some have become convinced the human condition is so depraved that the only thread of hope left is in the second advent of Christ. I believe in the visible return of our Lord. And, I believe, that when Christ does appear, the kingdom of God will be fully realized. However, I'm not ready to give up on the world. Not yet!

Standing on the Mount of Olives, the disciples asked, "Lord, will You at this time restore the kingdom to Israel?" That's a question many people are asking today. "When, Lord, will You come and deliver us out of this mess?" I believe what we need is to have the angel ask of us what he asked the disciples, "Why do you stand gazing up into heaven?" (v. 11) That's just another way of saying, "Don't give up, yet! God is not finished with the world!" To give up hope is to destine ourselves to futility and despair.

The Christian faith also gives us hope in the world beyond. These days we place an inordinate amount of interest in material and financial security. Every effort is made to make us feel secure and self-sufficient. Insurance policies, stocks, bonds, IRA's, and all our personal planning is designed to protect us from the accidental and inevitable. Yet, there is a curious paradox. With all of our planning and scheming, ours is the most neurotic generation on record. Is it any accident? Part of our neurosis and anxiety stems from the fact that we have lost a sense of hope in the world beyond. That is why we can be proud of the Christian faith. Its central message is that, in the death, burial, and resurrection of our Lord, death no longer writes the final line on the script of life.

Several months ago, I met Thurman in an oncology ward at a local hospital. He was in the latter stages of cancer and was given only a few days to live. We talked about dying and what that meant to both of us. Somewhere in the conversation, I asked, "Do you think about meeting God when death comes to you?"

"It seems to me that's all I've been thinking," he responded.

"Do you feel you're ready?" I asked.

"No," he responded with a despairing resignation.

"May I have your permission to tell you how to be ready?" I asked.

He nodded approvingly while staring at the bed sheets which covered his thin and deteriorating frame.

During the next several minutes, I had the privilege of sharing the Christian faith with him and, at the close, praying with him as he trusted Christ as his personal Savior and Lord.

When our praying ceased, I said, "Knowing the Christ of eternity is good, isn't it?"

"You bet it is!" he responded as we both rejoiced.

I never saw Thurman again. But, this I know: I will see him one day because I'm convinced the Christian faith answers our longing for immortality. "I am not ashamed of the gospel of Christ," exclaimed Paul. Neither am I. It produces what it promises. It meets all our needs. And, it prepares us for life here and beyond.

4

Through Discipleship

Enrolled in the
University of Heaven

(LUKE 14:25-33)

As a student there were two things I disliked about elementary school—lunches and report cards. Until the third grade, the lunches were great. Then, however, I learned with other students it was not in your best interest to like them.

Report cards, by nature, were not pleasant either. Their purpose was obvious enough: to point out where you should be academically by painfully reminding you of your present status. They were also designed to gently reprimand your parents for your poor performance. I'll never forget the time I was justly reprimanded by my parents when I tried to give my first *D* a penciled midsection in order to made it appear as a *B*. It didn't work.

Everyone knows what it is like to be in school. Some of you who read this are still in school. Others of you have long since closed that chapter in your life, while others may be contemplating going back to school. For me, my formal education ended in December 1986, when I graduated from seminary with the Doctor of Ministry degree. That was both a high and low moment in my life. The high you can imagine. The low I experienced resulted from a fundamental change in my life-style. For some twenty-five years, I had been in school uninterruptedly. Suddenly, I was no longer in school, and the new era in my life was difficult to manage. I remember wondering what having an advanced degree in theology could possibly mean. On the one hand, I felt fulfilled now that I was a "theologian," so to speak. On the other hand, I wondered about the value of such a costly personal investment. I discovered its value one evening, however, when I received a phone call that one of our parishioners had just given birth to a baby girl. I called the hospital to check on the condition of both mother and baby. Since it was late in the evening when I called, the switchboard operator was reluctant to put my call through to the patient's room. Hanging up the phone in frustration, I decided to call again and use my newly acquired identity as a "Dr."

"Hello," I said when the operator answered. "This is Dr. McSwain. Please connect me to the nurses' station on the maternity ward."

"Yes Sir," she replied without hesitation. Within minutes, I was talking to a nurse.

"Hi," I said. "This is Dr. McSwain. I'm calling to check on the status of a patient." And, I gave the nurse the patient's name.

"One moment," she kindly replied. "I'll go get her chart." Before I could explain that would not be necessary, she put me on hold. While I waited, I decided to play this thing to the finish and see what would happen. When the nurse returned, she began reading the patient's chart to me explaining and justifying all their medical procedures. I listened intently, occasionally responding with an "uh huh!" When she finished, I said, "Well, it sounds as if everything is in order. Now, please connect me with the patient herself."

"Yes, Sir," doctor!" she replied. Hesitating momentarily, she continued, "By the way, doctor, are you the pediatrician or the obstetrician?"

"Neither," I replied, "I'm the theologian!"

"Oh!" she responded somewhat perplexed. I can imagine she's still trying to figure out what kind of doctor I am. Nonetheless, I am no longer questioning the significance of my educational pursuits. There are some benefits to holding an advanced degree.

If there is anything I have learned over the years it is that learning never ends. In many ways, life is a school. And, from a Christian perspective, being a follower of Christ is like being enrolled in an institution of higher learning.

We have many names for Jesus. He is called Christ, Lord, Savior, Messiah, and so forth. One of His designations we seldom contemplate, however, is the title *Rabbi*, which means teacher. If Christ is our *Teacher*, then we are His disciples or "students." As His student, we are enrolled in His school.

I think the church needs to promote this concept because we are living in a time when being a Christian is more like a spectator sport than a participatory enterprise. For example, one interesting phenomenon is taking place in the church today. On the one hand, while we are seeking to construct huge edifices and gather great masses of people together in one place, Jesus, on the other hand, sought to whittle away at the great number of people who followed Him in order to gather a faithful few. In our text, Jesus was perhaps at the apex of His popularity. He had a huge following (see Luke 14:16-25). The thing which would bolster the egos of most ministers today was the very thing which bothered Jesus the most. He seemed more interested in a few following faithfully than in many following flippantly or casually. That's the point of the twin parables of the man who began to build a tower but was unable to finish (vv. 28-30) and the king who went to make war against another king but was ill-prepared for the challenge (vv. 31-32). The problem was that neither seriously counted the cost before engaging in the task. It would be like a student enrolling in a college course before contemplating the demands of the curriculum.

Every follower of Christ needs to seriously consider the course requirements before casually enrolling in the University of Heaven. "What is expected of me if I become a student in Christ's school?" is a good question to ask of yourself. What is expected? Jesus provides the answers. Consider them.

Relationships

"If anyone comes to Me," said Jesus, "and does not hate his father and mother, wife and children, brothers and sisters, yes, and his own life also he cannot be My disciple" (v. 26). How could He who told us to love our enemies (Matt. 5:44) now tell us to hate our families? That's not an easy question to answer. However, I believe the issue here is one of loyalty in relationships. It is interesting to me how people invest their loyalties. You can frequently identify people's loyalties by how they invest their time and resources. Consider the following paradox. Some people will risk driving through a blizzard to maintain a loyalty to an athletic club but: At the first sign of a few flurries, however, many of these same people will not drive to church to demonstrate loyalty to Christ and His people in worship. Jesus is saying, "Whoever comes to Me cannot be My disciple unless he loves Me more than _____." You fill in the blank. Do you love Christ more than your family, friends, or ambitions? If you love your family more than Christ, what do you do if your family is irreligious?

Recently, I talked with a ninety-year-old woman in our community who shared the frustrating story of her spiritual history. As a teenager she started attending church, even though her parents had forbidden her to go. She slipped away from home to attend church frequently only to be found out and whipped for it by her irreligious father. Wielding his ruthless authority as her father, he made it virtually impossible for her to attend. One day, however, she bravely confronted him by saying, "You may keep me from church, but you will never keep me from Christ."

Fortunately, most of us will never have to make that kind of choice between family and Christ. But, what would you do if you did? Jesus is to hold the place of supreme loyalty in our lives over anything or anyone else.

What about your friends, peers, or colleagues? Do you find yourself compromising your loyalty to Christ in order to "fit in" with those at school or work? What about the dreams and ambitions you have for life? Are they your dreams solely? Or, are they the dreams Christ has for your life? These, too, are difficult questions for any of us to answer. What bothers me, however, is that so few seriously wrestle with these issues.

I'm not sure but we may have made following Christ all too easy. We seem more interested in graduating people before they've ever enrolled in Christ's school. Being caught up in a "numbers game," we have made it easier to join a local church than it is to join a local civic club. I'm sure you have seen, as I have, the bumper sticker "Honk, if you love Jesus." Recently, however, I saw one that draws a more challenging distinction: "If you love Jesus, tithe, any-body can honk!" I'm not suggesting that tithing is the mark of disci-pleship, but I do believe we have softened the claims of Christ upon our lives until we now have what Bonhoeffer called "cheap grace."

Ray Kroc, founder of the McDonalds' empire, was once asked by a reporter, "What do you believe in?"

Without hesitation, he responded, "God, family, and Mc-Donalds!" Then, pausing, he continued, "But, I must confess, when I get to the office on Monday morning, I reverse the order!" He's not the only person who lives by one set of loyalties on Sunday and a different set of loyalties on Monday. If someone were to observe the way you spend your time, invest your resources, and expend your energies, what would he likely conclude is the ultimate loyalty of your life?

The kind of loyalty Jesus looks for from His followers is best seen in the life of a man I met a few years ago. I was conducting a series of services at a church in Augusta, Georgia, when one eve-ning following the service, Dr. Mercer Bridges, a retired orthopedic surgeon and member of the church, introduced me to a man whose arms had been severed in an accident. Working on a combine ma-chine one arm got caught in its ruthless jaws. As he tried to free himself, his other arm got caught in its grip and, within seconds, both arms were severed at his shoulders. As his surgeon, Bridges tried to surgically reattach his arms but the damage was too severe. He would have to live the rest of his life with artificial arms and hands. "The amazing thing about all of this," explained Dr. Bridges, "is that, when he came out of surgery, the very first thing he said to our minister was, 'Pastor, I don't think I'll be able to make it to church Sunday, could you help me find someone to teach my Sun-day School class?'" I believe it is this kind of selfless loyalty to Christ that Jesus expects of every follower.

Crossbearing

What is expected of each of us who would follow Jesus? In verse 27, Jesus said, "And whoever does not bear his cross and come after Me cannot be My disciple." What does it mean to bear one's cross?

Once, I heard two women talking. "How are you feeling these days?" asked one. The other responded by describing all her aches and pains. "Well," explained the first, "You know what the Bible says—we must all bear our own cross!"

Is this what Jesus meant by bearing your cross? No! All people, Christian and on-Christian, experience human suffering. It's part of the price we pay to be members of the human family.

Crossbearing refers to our willingness to take a stand for Christ when it would be easier to go along with the tide of popular opinion. A few years ago, my family and I were walking through a huge mall in Louisville, Kentucky. Passing a fast food restaurant, I suggested we buy our lunch. As we were preparing to leave, my attention turned to a sign which stood at the entrance of the restaurant which read: "It is our nationwide policy to be closed on Sunday. Thank you for allowing us to serve you Monday through Saturday." I stood there for a moment thinking back to the days when all stores closed on Sunday. I was jolted back to the present, however, when the waitress ran over and said, "Sir, is there something wrong?"

"No!" I responded. "I was just thinking about how unusual it is to find a place of business that closes on Sunday."

"Oh, you have to understand," she explained, "The man who owns this chain of restaurants is one of those religious types!" I later learned the man she was referring to is a Christian businessman.

"Well," I said in response to her, "I'm glad there are a few people in our society for whom the dollar is not as 'Almighty' as most people think!"

I am not suggesting that we go back to those days when all stores closed on Sunday or that discipleship is defined in such a manner. But, I do think bearing your cross has something to do with giving witness to your faith in Christ when it is unpopular and, as in this illustration, unprofitable to do so.

Bearing your cross also means to voluntarily suffer for another human to help alleviate the other's pain and suffering and point them in the direction of the kingdom of God.

Several years ago, a hurricane swept across the island of Puerto Rico devastating property and taking the lives of many people. Two persons responded to the disaster in entirely different ways. One was Howard Hughes, a man of immeasurable wealth. When he heard weather warnings of the approaching storm, he left his penthouse suite in Puerto Rico, boarded his private plane, and flew to safety. The other response to the disaster was from Roberto Clemente, star player for the Pittsburg Pirates. When Clemente learned of the wake of devastation left by the hurricane, he chartered a plane at his own expense, gathered as many relief supplies as he could, and delivered those resources to his battered homeland. On the return flight, his plane crashed. News reporters commented about the tragedy of Roberto Clemente losing his life. But, they were wrong. Clemente sacrificially gave his life in service of others.

To be a follower of Christ means to bear your cross for others just as Christ did for each of us.

Renunciation

There's one other thing Jesus expects of all who would enroll in the University of Heaven. "So likewise, whoever of you does not forsake all that he has cannot be My disciple" (v. 33). "Forsake all?" Did Jesus really mean that? I heard someone recently refer to this as a hyperbole, an intentional exaggeration by Jesus in order to make a point. Perhaps it is. But, what bothers me is how Christians try to water down the stringent demands of Jesus.

Nothing is to take the place of the preeminence of Christ and His will in our lives. To forsake all means to take everything you are and you have and place it in the service of Christ and His kingdom.

This is the one thing the rich young ruler was unwilling to do. He asked Jesus, "Good Teacher, what shall I do that I may inherit eternal life?" (Mark 10:17).

Jesus reiterated the commandments and the young man responded, "Teacher, all these I have observed from my youth" (v. 20).

"One thing you lack," said Jesus, "Go your way, sell whatever you have and give to the poor" (v. 21). And, the Bible says that he "went away grieved, for he had great possessions" (v. 22). The truth is: great possessions had him. Is there anything you are withholding from Christ? The thing we withhold from Christ is the very thing that keeps us from Christ. The things we possess, if not surrendered to Christ, become the things that possess us.

Several years ago, I heard the story of an eight-year-old-boy in upstate New York who emptied his piggy bank one Saturday and announced to his father that he wanted a ride to a local bakery so he could purchase 200 loaves of bread.

"What have you done?" his perplexed father shouted.

"Well," he explained, "I just heard on the radio that the bakery was selling day-old bread for ten cents a loaf and I've got twenty dollars to buy it."

"But, why would you want to do that?" his father pressed.

"Don't you remember, Daddy?" he explained. "Last Sunday, the pastor told us of all the poor people in Africa, and I just wanted to help!"

Somewhat reluctantly, the boy's father took him to the bakery whereupon he purchased 200 loaves of bread and loaded them in the family station wagon. Then the father proceeded to drive the boy and the bread to the minister's home. When they arrived, the man said to his minister, "Look what you've started!" and explained their dilemma. "What should we do with all this bread? And, how can we possibly send it to Africa?"

"I've got an idea," said the minister. "Take it over to the church, display it on a table in the vestibule, and be sure to be in church tomorrow morning."

During the worship hour the next day, the pastor reminded the congregation of his sermon the week before. Then he said, "Folks, there is one young man in our church who took the message seriously and decided to try to do something about it. You will find 200 loaves of bread on a table in the church vestibule, and after the service, you are invited to purchase a loaf for ten dollars."

At the close of the service, the little boy stood behind the table of bread and sold each loaf as the parishioners exited. When the last loaf was sold, the boy was proudly holding 2,000 dollars in his hands. Soon thereafter he sent the money to a relief organization in Africa.

Being a follower of Christ means that we take all we are and have, give it to Jesus, and let Him multiply it and use it in service of others and His kingdom.

What are the curriculum requirements in the University of Heaven? Your loyalty to Christ must take precedence over all other loyalties and relationships. Take up your own cross and follow Jesus. Give Jesus *all* your life and let Him use your gifts and resources in His kingdom work. Believe me, neither you nor Christ will be disappointed with the outcome.

5
Through Mission

On Knowing Why We're Here

(JONAH 1—4)

A religion editor of a well-known newspaper once raised a question worth probing. "What is the test of a great church?" He answered himself with yet another question. "If the church disappeared, would anyone miss it besides the members?"[1] The question is interesting. It challenges us to examine the reasons for the church's existence. It invites us to consider how well the church is doing at fulfilling its purpose and mission.

In recent months, I've been captivated by the story of Jonah. I believe the church's purpose and mission is addressed in that short story as well, if not better, than any other place in all of Holy Scripture.

Jonah is the most New Testament-like book we have in the Old Testament. It's a story not just about a rebellious preacher out of the past but about religious people in the present. Sometimes I wonder if we in the contemporary church are prepared for the radical message of Jonah. Because it is controversial, some have watered down its message. For some it has been relegated to the status of a fairy tale about a whale that swallows a man. It is my hope, however, that the church will rehear its message. Its message is the mission of the church. This short story contains an answer to the question about the purpose of the church. The way the church responds to the message of Jonah will determine whether the church will be missed in any community were it to suddenly disappear.

The Mission Revealed

The first words that come to Jonah are: "Arise, go to Nineveh" (Jonah 1:2). That is like saying, "Get up and get busy." Jonah was stunned to say the least. "What do you mean?" Jonah reacted. "Nineveh? You've got to be kidding!" Of course, we know that Jews despised Ninevites. Nineveh was the capital of Assyria. It was one of the most powerful and wicked nations on earth at that time. As a result, Nineveh was not considered a mission field to the Jews. In fact, the Ninevites were considered beyond the reach of God's redemptive grace. H. Stephen Shoemaker has reminded us that over the years we have changed the name of Nineveh ". . . to Babylon, to Rome, to Berlin, to Moscow, Havana, and Iran. Nineveh is the land where godless people live and threaten to take us over."[2] Nineveh, however, does not have to be some far-off land. It might be your next-door neighbor. You see, Nineveh is any place where you refuse to engage in the mission of God.

It is amazing how often we draw boundaries around the grace of God and mission work of the church. There are 100 million people in the United States who are unaffiliated with any religious group. Of the 40,000-plus people who reside in the county in which I live, over half are unaffiliated with any church. I sometimes feel like asking if we consider these to be within the reach of God's grace? How often do our arms of love embrace the "Ninevites" who live in our own neighborhoods?

"Who will win America?" was the theme slogan in a recent mission emphasis of one denomination. It's a good question. Who will?

Jeff and Melva Clark returned from a mission trip to Kenya. Jeff made a startling observation in a mission report. He said, "We have it all wrong in our churches in America. We think God occasionally calls an individual to enter missions. What we should understand, however, is that God has called everyone into Christian missions *unless* He indicates otherwise." Perhaps it would make an incredible difference in evangelizing the world if churches would emphasize the fact that God calls all persons into missions. And, in those instances where He directs otherwise, he still calls all persons to be missionaries in their efforts to reach others. You may be an employee in a factory, but you are also a missionary. You may be a schoolteacher, but you are also a missionary. You may be a housewife, doctor, lawyer, or self-employed mechanic, but you are also a missionary.

We talk about church growth. But, when we're honest we have to admit that most church growth is little more than the transferring of church memberships and baptizing of the children of church members. Church Growth Consultant Ron Lewis was conducting a growth conference in which he was quoted as saying, "In 92% of your churches the only real growth you've had in the last five years has been from baptizing the children of your members and from transfers of members from other churches."[3] Somehow, someway, the church must understand that an "unmissionary Christianity is a contradiction of terms."[4]

The Mission Refused

Jonah refused to go. That's not the first time in history people have refused to do what God requires them to do.

In a meeting where the mission of the church was being discussed, one deacon revealed more of his personal theology than he was aware when he said, "My next door neighbor sees us get up every Sunday and go to church. He knows where we are, and if he wants to come, he knows where to find us."

I thought to myself, *Whatever happened to "Go therefore and make disciples" (Matthew 28:19), and "Go out into the highways and hedges, and compel them to come in, that my house may be filled" (Luke 14:23)?*

Instead of going to Nineveh, Jonah took a ship to Tarshish. God said, "Go east," and Jonah went west. As he journeyed, a storm arose. The sailors were scared half out of their wits. They cast lots to find out whose god as mad at whom. The lot fell on Jonah. They went to him and found him sleeping in the hull of the ship. "All right, sailor, what's going on with you?" they demanded.

Jonah confessed he was running from the Lord and instructed them, "Throw me overboard and your lives may be spared!" Notice, however, verses 12 and 13. They tried compassionately to avoid Jonah's suggestion. It is interesting to me that they displayed more concern for the physical safety of Jonah than Jonah displayed for the spiritual salvation of the Ninevites. I suppose that's the sad thing about this story and our story. Few people are being converted these days because few of us seem concerned to urge them to believe in the kingdom of grace.

One man asked me, "Do church folk really care that people are lost, without Christ?" To answer his question truthfully is painful. I know how easy it is for all of us to be care-less about that matter.

The harder the sailors rowed the more intense the storm became. So, when the sailors grew weary of rowing, they tossed Jonah over the side of the boat. And then, the part about the whale comes into the picture. I think sometimes we get "hooked" by the fish and miss the message of the story and role the fish plays in it.

As an old country preacher used to say, "Jonah is a high-tailin' it from God." He is trying to hide from God and avoid His bidding to go to Nineveh. From the turbulent waves around him, Jonah rests safely in the belly of the fish.

If spiritualizing a text is ever acceptable, today we might call the whale, the church. It's easy for us to hide within the interior of the church and avoid "what it's here for." From the turbulent world around us, the church becomes the safest and often he least-threatening environment. Within a barrage of church activities, it is easy to hide from God and avoid His calling to go to Nineveh. It's true, isn't it?

Often our worship exposes our incongruous nature. We sing hymns like "Bringing in the Sheaves," when most of us have had to drag ourselves out of bed just to get to church. We sing "Make Me a Channel of Blessing," when most of us would rather be changing channels on our TV looking for something interesting. Or, we sing "We've a Story to Tell to the Nations," when really it's more fun to share gossip we've just savored. Then, there is the challenging song, "Take My Life and Let It Be"—and what we really mean by that is let it be comfortable, convenient, peaceful, and undisturbed. "Don't bother me, Lord! Just let me be."

We are like the drunk who staggered down the sidewalk, tripped, and fell backwards into some freshly poured concrete. Unable to get up, he felt the concrete ooze around his drunken frame and harden. When he was discovered the next morning, firefighters were called upon to come and free him from the hardened concrete. Every time the sledge hammer crashed against the pavement his body rattled with pain. When finally freed, he stood slowly and was overheard mumbling, "Getting drunk is all right in the abstract, but it ain't much in the concrete!" That's the problem many of us have. It is so much easier to be abstract about the church's mission than it is to be concrete about the church's mission in the world.

While it seems safe to hide from our mission inside the church, God won't let us stay there. If it is true that God comforts the afflicted and afflicts the comfortable, then he will do to us what He did to Jonah. He will cause the fish to spit us upon the shores of reality. Don't ever believe God will let the church drift passively over a sea of turmoil. He'll never let us pull that one off. Within the span of three days, Jonah found himself on the shore. Was he any different? Probably not! H. Stephen Shoemaker is insightful and humorous: "The whale changed Jonah's *destination* but not his *disposition*. It changed Jonah's *geography* but not his *theology*."[5]

The Mission Reaffirmed

God's word came to Jonah a second time, and interestingly, it was the same word. "Arise, go to Nineveh" (3:2). God's mission never changes. Some of us have heard it all our lives. We have heard it so much we no longer hear it. It may not be true that "familiarity breeds contempt," but it is true that "familiarity breeds indifference." We've grown indifferent to the mission of the church, have we not?

There is hope. The second time around, Jonah went. And, at first, we are encouraged. Jonah prepares to have had a change of heart. He seems to have reluctantly accepted his God-given mission. Don't get too excited, however. Look at his sermon. "Yet forty days, and Nineveh shall be overthrown!" (v. 4). His sermon reveals the attitude of his heart. He's not there because he wants to be there. He's there out of a sense of obligation and a spirit of vengeance. He's there because he can't win with God. He's like a lot of Christians I know. He's doing God's work not because he wants to, but because he feels he has no choice. Jonah is angry at the Ninevites and his preaching reflects his desire to get revenge. He is not the first preacher who has ever used the pulpit to vent anger or even seek revenge. He hopes God will stomp on them like some good church folks hope God will trample their enemies. However, it didn't turn out as Jonah had hoped. When the Ninevites heard Jonah shout his obscenities and judgments, strangely God's grace was mediated and the people repented. Sometimes, I'm amazed at what God is able to do with my feeble efforts at proclaiming His grace, especially when there's little grace in my heart (or the tone of my voice). And, I'm amazed at what He's able to do with the church's witness for Christ, even when our attitudes are not right. Few of us would be inclined to pat ourselves on the back for being "super-Christians." Yet, God is able to work through us, and sometimes, He does in spite of us.

How did Jonah react when the Ninevites repented? The answer is found in 4:1-2. "But it displeased Jonah exceedingly, and he became angry." (Of course, Jonah was already angry. But now, he's really mad.) "So he prayed to the Lord, 'Ah, Lord, was not this what I said when I was still in my country?'" That's like saying: "I told you so! I said you were a gracious, forgiving God. I knew you wouldn't destroy them. I preached judgment, and you've shown mercy. That's not fair. I preached hell-fire-and-damnation, and you've responded with love and affirmation. I won't take it. You won't make me out to be a fool." The rebukes flowed freely from Jonah's wounded pride.

Jonah walked away sulking. His behavior reminds me of other persons I've known who have walked out on God, the church, or a marriage, when things didn't turn out as hoped. But there, in the middle of his sniffles, God caused a plant to grow over his head to provide shade for him. Jonah was grateful for the plant. It was a peaceful experience for him. It's amazing, but God knows there are times we need to be still and think about His activity and, sometimes, His inactivity in our lives.

However, Jonah's heart was still not right. He had much to

learn. So, when morning came, a worm appeared and ate away the life of the plant much like a termite might eat away the foundation of a house, only much faster. Jonah was furious. With a wrinkled brown and his face aflame with anger, he said, "How could you let this happen, God? You're so difficult to understand! Here you let 120,000 of the most wicked people in the world live and let my lovely plant die!"

In essence, God gingerly responds, "Jonah, you are the one who is difficult to understand. You display more concern for your plant than you display for my people. I am more concerned about people than any plant."

The story ends on that word. We're left wondering if it is not easier for some of us to shed tears over a fern plant that dies in the sun room than we shed for the people of the world who are dying without the "Sonshine" of Christ radiating in their hearts.

The story of Jonah leaves each of us with a decision. Will we rejoice in the grace of God that extends to all people and share in the spreading of that grace? Or will we pout, as did Jonah, over the grace God freely offers to all?

In was Monday night basketball for men over thirty at our church. I was there not because I'm much of a basketball player but because I like the game and enjoy the fellowship with several of the men. At halftime, a faithful member approached me and asked about a man whose name had appeared on our church prayer list for several weeks. Under any other circumstances, that would not be unusual. This time, however, the man whose name had appeared on our prayer list was, at one time, the Grand Wizard of the Ku Klux Klan (KKK).

The tone of his voice and the manner of his question signaled to me the church member was obviously disturbed that his name appeared on the prayer list. I explained to the member that I had been visiting the man ever since his near fatal accident which had left him incapacitated.

"Has he demonstrated any visible sign of repentance?" the member asked firmly.

"Well, I believe so," I responded somewhat hesitantly. "My impression is that he's trying to find God, turn loose of his prejudice, and put his past behind him."

"Umph!" he snorted with an obvious disbelief. "It sure seems weird to me," he explained, "but I guess if the Ayatollah Khomeini were to repent, forgiveness would be available to him, too!" As he spoke, I thought about Jonah and the Ninevites and the grace of God which reaches out in forgiveness even to members of the KKK.

How will we accept the words of God, "Arise and go?" Willingly? Or begrudgingly? You see, Jonah is not some obscure figure of antiquity; Jonah is you. Jonah is me. And, until the rebellious Jonah in each of our hearts has been confronted, the mission of the church is at a standstill.

The question begs for an answer. "If the church were to suddenly disappear, would anyone miss it besides the members?" The answer to that question depends upon the manner and seriousness with which each of us accepts our mission in the world. Our response determines the impact the church has on individual communities and, ultimately, the world. Emil Brunner, the German theologian, was right when he said that the church exists by mission as fire exists by burning. Without a grateful acceptance of the mission of God, the church ceases to be the church. With it, however, the church becomes a reconciled Jonah, reconciling the world.

6
Through Triumph
Life's Arenas of Victory
(2 CORINTHIANS 2:5-16)

Someone once said: "Most people admire a good loser—as long as it's somebody else." It's true, isn't it? We savor victory. From the Little League baseball game to the corporate takeover on Wall Street, the name of the game is to win. The apostle Paul expressed our sentiments when he said: "Now thanks be to God who always leads us in triumph in Christ" (v. 14). With our bent toward winning, we enjoy promises like that. But, the declaration of Paul asks the question: "Into what arenas of life does God lead us in triumph?" It is important to know since there's a great deal of confusion about it. The preaching that's popular today is the kind that promises people "outrageous fortune." However, it would serve us well to reexamine those arenas wherein we may truly experience victory.

Recently, I heard about two big city coaches who went north to ice fish. Having purchased all the required paraphernalia at a sporting goods store—lines, poles, lures, bait, and a small power saw to cut through the ice—they found their location, pitched a tent, and proceeded to cut a hole in the ice.

Just as they got started, however, they heard a voice call out, "There's no fish under the ice." They looked at each other startled and wondered where the voice was coming from. Then, they proceeded with their work. Again, the voice called out, "There's no fish under the ice." Both looked up thinking the voice was coming from above and returned to their work pretending they didn't hear it. The voice thundered a third time.

Finally, one coach could stand it no longer. He stood up and cried out, "Is that you, Lord?"

"No," returned the voice. "This is the manager of the ice-skating arena!"

God may lead us in triumph, but it is important to identify the arenas of life where victory may honestly be experienced. Fortunately, the apostle Paul does not leave us guessing. He clearly identifies those arenas in the passage before us. Observe them and then begin to experience victory for yourself.

Relationships

It is impossible to read 2 Corinthians 2:1-11 without receiving the distinct impression there was a serious relational flaw among the Corinthian Christians. Nobody knows for certain what the exact nature of the problem was. However, in 1 Corinthians 5, we learn of a member of the congregation who was guilty of incest. Perhaps that is the problem to which Paul alludes in the passage before us. In any case, it is noteworthy that the early church took seriously the matter of disciplining errant members. Apparently, the Corinthians had exercised some sort of discipling action against the person or persons responsible for infecting the church's spirit of internal harmony and external witness in the world. Therefore, Paul said, in essence, "Enough is enough!" He instructed,

> This punishment which was inflicted by the majority is sufficient for such a man, so that, on the contrary, you ought rather to forgive and comfort him, lest perhaps such a one be swallowed up with too much sorrow. Therefore, I urge you to reaffirm your love to him (vv. 6-8).

Dealing with people in general is tough enough. Dealing with problem people is next to impossible. Whenever I think about getting along with people, I recall an essay a little girl was asked to write entitled "People."

> People are composed of girls and boys, also men and women. Boys are no good at all until they grow up and get married. Men who don't get married are no good either. Boys are an awful bother. My mother is a woman, and my father is a man. A woman is a grown-up

girl with children. My father is such a nice man, that I think he must
have been a girl when he was a boy![1]

The essay captures the complexity of human relationships. We
all become a little tongue-tied and confused when it comes to understanding and getting along with people. Yet, Scripture holds out the
promise that each of us may triumph in Christ in the arena of our
human relationships. They key to experiencing this victory is in
modeling the way Christ dealt with people.

Jesus treated all people with dignity. He believed everyone was
of equal worth. While people are hardly equal in gifts as the parable
of the talents makes clear (Matt. 25:14-30), they are of equal significance as the story of the Samaritan woman illustrates (John 4). We
make the complexity of our own relationships all the more complex
when we attach degrees of significance to people based on color,
class, or condition.

In addition to this, humility is an attitude Jesus cultivated in all
His relationships. In learning to triumph in this arena, it might help
to humbly remember that, while we talk about the difficult people
with whom we live and work, sometimes we are those difficult people ourselves. Think about how offensive Jesus was to many of the
people of His day (Mark 6:1-6). It may help you to humbly accept
your own offensiveness to others and keep you from being on the
defensive.

In all of Jesu's actions with people and reactions to people, His
aim was always conciliatory. Even in His stern rebukes of the religious establishment, He held out hope of redeeming people and
even prayed for that to happen. Read the "Woes" passage in Matthew 23. Notice, however, how the chapter ends with Jesus praying,
"O Jerusalem, Jerusalem. . . . How often I wanted to gather your
children together" (v. 37). Sometimes, the pain of confrontation is
preferred over the ease of silence. In any event, since Christ has led
the way toward our own reconciliation to God, can we attempt anything less in our relationship with others? Keep the promise before
you: "Now thanks be to God who always leads us in triumph in
Christ" in the arena of human relationships.

Choices

"Furthermore," said Paul, "When I came to Troas to preach Christ's gospel, and a door was opened unto me of the Lord, I had no rest in my spirit" (vv. 12-13). The apostle is letting us in on his struggles. Troas was the northwesternmost city in Asia Minor (modern-day Turkey). Paul had traveled all the way from Ephesus to this coastal city when God opened a door of opportunity for him. Yet, he could find no peace in his heart at the thought of stepping through that door. Why? Because he could not find his Christian brother Titus (v. 13). So, he chose another door of opportunity and departed for Macedonia.

Here is a man struggling between two alternatives. I know about this struggle. I suspect you do, too. Sometimes, I think we look at the apostle Paul as if he were a super-Christian for whom life always worked out perfectly with little effort. I have news for you, however. Life was not effortless for Paul. He struggled between choices in life just as you and I do.

All of life is made up of choices. I become a little uneasy around people who seem to make choices so effortlessly. It has never been easy for me and I suspect, if the truth were known, we all struggle with the alternatives life lays before us.

In deciding upon which college to attend, what career to pursue, and whom to marry (to mention a few of the choices we must make in life), I think it helps to ask both investigative and intuitive questions. What impact will this choice have upon my life? my family? What are the pros and cons of both choices? And, how do I feel about choosing this or that path?

For the Christian, of course, there is always the consideration of God's will. Which path does He want me to take? Rather than simplifying the decisions we must make, I think that seeking the will of God can be a complex process. I hear people testify that God spoke to them telling them both what to say and do in various situations of life. That has never been my experience. I often struggle to know God's will in the choices of life. There have even been times I've had to make decisions when, after much prayer and reflection, I was still a little uncertain as to the will of God for my life.

There are two things I have come to believe. One is that God truly leads us in triumph in the choices we make in life. Sometimes, however, the triumph is experienced as we look back on life and see how the hand of God has guided us. The other is that, when we make wrong choices, and all of us have at times, God is still able to use us wherever and in whatever circumstances we find ourselves.

The one-time White House "hatchet" man Charles Colson, who was convicted in the Watergate scandal and sent to prison, was used by God in spite of the foolish choices he had made early in his life. While serving time in prison, he was dramatically converted, and God gave him a vision of a path down which he could travel to a life of usefulness and productivity. Today, Colson operates the most successful and far-reaching prison ministry in the United States. "Now thanks be to God who always leads us in triumph in Christ" in the choices we make through life. He will lead you, and you must believe that. Don't expect it to be an easy or simple process.

Eternity

The most compelling triumph we experience in Christ is in the arena of eternity. The apostle wrote,

> Now thanks be to God . . . who through us diffuses the fragrance of His knowledge in every place. For we are to God the fragrance of His knowledge in every place. For we are to God the fragrance of Christ among those who are being saved and among those who are perishing. To the one we are the aroma of death to death, and to the other the aroma of life to life (vv. 14-16).

Paul employed the image of the Roman army to illustrate the victory that is ours in eternity. Whenever a commander of the Roman army marched into the city after experiencing victory at battle, all of his soldiers and subjects would march in a victory parade. Some would carry flasks of burning incense and the fragrance would fill the air. To the soldiers of victory the fragrance was a sweet aroma. To the soldiers of defeat who were led into captivity, however, it was the stench of death.

Paul borrowed this familiar scene and applied it spiritually to our triumph in Christ. Jesus defeated death in His resurrection and now the fragrance of victory fills the air for every believer. It is impossible to march through life with a sense of victory without faith in the Christ who has defeated death in the arena of eternity. When, however, you have settled the issue of your eternal destiny, you will be like the fellow who stayed up late one evening to watch the replay of a basketball game on television. Having heard earlier in the day that his favored team won the game, he sat through the replay with little emotion in spite of the fact that his team trailed by ten points through most of the game. How could he be so calm? Because he knew the final outcome of the game.

Christians may experience defeat in many arenas of life. However, for the Christian, there's the scent of victory filling the air due to the fact that Christ has won the final battle for us. His victory assures our victory. His triumph ensures our triumph over sin, death, and eternity.

Recently, I clipped an article from a newspaper entitled, "Hawkings' Race Against Time." It is the story of Stephen Hawkings, author of the best-selling book *A Brief History of Time*. Hawkings holds a doctorate in theoretical astronomy from Cambridge University and is regarded by many as the greatest thinker of our time. His mind has been compared to that of Albert Einstein. However, at only forty-seven years of age, Hawkings is confined to a wheelchair and paralyzed by Lou Gehrig's disease. Unable to speak, he communicates with the assistance of a computer attached to his wheelchair.

Like Einstein who came before him, Hawkings does not believe in God. Knowing his life expectancy is short at best, he says, "I always feel I'm in a race against time . . . I've been successful in my work. I have a beautiful family and I've written a best-seller. One can't hope for much more!"[2]

With all due respect, I must disagree with Hawkings's conclusions about what any of us may hope for in life and death. Like him, I believe we should cram as much of life as we can in the time we have on this earth. But, to hope for little more than a good job, family, and best-seller is pretty depressing. Someone once said, "He who has no hope in the future has no hold on today!" This is why the Christian gospel is so exhilarating. With the apostle Paul, we may boldly declare, "Now thanks be to God who always leads us in triumph in Christ" in the arena of eternity. In Christ, everlasting life is an eternal reality.

God is a God of triumph and victory. More than anything else, He wants each of us to experience His victory in the arena of our relationships in life, choices through life, and destiny at the end of life. Celebrate life's arenas of victory. The battle has been won already!

7
Through Stewardship
Examining Our Motives
for Giving

(2 CORINTHIANS 9:1-15)

A man once said to his pastor, "I've had it! All you preachers ever talk about is giving, giving, giving, and more giving!"

"Thank you," responded the minister. "That's the best definition of Christianity I've ever heard." I can't say much about the sensitivity of the minister's pastoral response, but I could speak volumes about the minister's understanding of the Christian faith.

Every Christian should give. The time should come when the subject of giving need not be defended with those who've been members of the Christian church for many years. When Paul wrote to the Corinthian church he said, "Now concerning the [service] to the saints, it is superfluous for me to write to you" (2 Cor. 9:1). Paul says it's not necessary for him to write about giving, yet he writes anyway. So much of the preaching and teaching that goes on in the church is superfluous. It's often just a repeat of what Christians ought to know already and be doing regularly. Giving is just one of those superfluous subjects. Christians ought to be giving and should not have to be reminded every few weeks or months to do what should be natural and spontaneous.

Explore with me three questions: (1) Why *don't* some people give? (2) Why *do* some people give? (3) And, why *should* we give?

Why Don't Some People Give?

Some people do not give because they have never been taught to give. This is the place where we must begin, although it is not the category in which the typical Christian would fall. If you've grown up in a church it is highly probable you have been taught to give.

It is conceivable, however, there are some who've never had the opportunity of being taught the joy of giving. Nor have they ever had good role models with regard to giving. For example, there are some who come to church regularly but do not regularly give, and when they do, it is far less than a tithe (a tenth) of their earnings. Such persons are certainly not the best role models for young churchgoers and children, particularly their own children. We have a whole generation of church members who do not give because they've never been taught to give by their primary care givers—their parents and others.

Learning to tithe is caught more than taught. Therefore, in exploring reasons why some do not give, we have to come to terms with the fact that some have never been taught to give, either by example or by explanation.

A second reason as to why some do not give is because they simply refuse to give. Any serious look at reasons why most church folk do not give would be incomplete without taking into consideration the matter of their willingness or their "want to." There are many who know what the tithe is. They know God expects them to give. The problem is not a lack of knowledge but a lack of willingness.

They remind me of the fellow who was visited by members of a church building committee. They went to enlist him in the program of giving. After their budget presentation, the man said, "I see you have done your research, but let me ask you a couple of questions. Do you know that I have a widowed mother who has no visible means of support?"

"No!" they responded with some surprise.

He continued, "Do you know that I have a sister whose drunken husband has walked off and left her and five children, and they have no other means of support?" Without batting an eye, he continued, "And do you know that I have a brother who was hurt in an automobile accident and is paralyzed and will never work another day of his life?"

By now the committee was feeling anxious and wishing they were anywhere but there. "Well," the man finished triumphantly, "if

I've never done anything to help them, what makes you think I'll do anything to help you?"

The attitude he expressed is all too familiar in the church. Some people refuse to give, and regardless of what you may say to them, their attitude about it remains the same.

Remember the story of the widow's mite? One frustrated preacher said that he decided to call the offering plates in his church the "mite plates" because the people in his congregation "might" put something in them or they might not.

A few weeks ago a story appeared in a newspaper about a man who wanted his $61 tax refund from the IRS. Instead, however, he received $10,000 back from the IRS. An official with the IRS said if he had cashed the check, the government would probably never have caught the mistake.

The man was quoted as saying, "I was tempted to try to find a way to keep it!" He's not the only person who has ever been tempted to keep what doesn't belong to him. Christians do that all the time with their tithes and offerings.

I've been teaching Jonathan, my six-year-old son, the importance of giving. One Sunday morning, I gave him a quarter and instructed him to put it in the Sunday School offering. As I was turning on the lights and checking the thermostats in the Sunday School rooms, Jonathan approached me excitedly and said, "Daddy, can I have a dime?"

"What for?" I asked, knowing he had just emerged from the activities building where the soda machine is located.

"I want to buy a grape drink," he explained. "See, I have a quarter and all I need is a dime."

"Where did you get that quarter?" I asked, not because I was in the dark as to its origin, but because I wanted him to admit it was his tithe money I had given him that morning.

He dropped his head and said, "It's the quarter you gave me for the Sunday School offering." My mind turned immediately to the thought that there must be scores of well-meaning people who knowingly take what belongs to the Lord and selfishly spend it on things for themselves.

These are at least a couple of reasons why some people do not give. Some have never been taught to give and others simply refuse to give. If there are some who don't give, what motivates those who do? Why *do* some people give?

Why Do Some People Give?

There are some who give in order to receive, a kind of "You scratch my back, and I'll scratch yours" arrangement with God. Look at verse 6. We misread this verse sometimes. For example, I heard one preacher say, "If you want to make a million dollars, give God one hundred thousand." It doesn't take a mental heavyweight to figure out what he believes. He believes God is obligated to reward him when he gives. That is not what the apostle Paul meant by his words because; if so, why are there countless persons who have given regularly and faithfully over the years and, yet, they've never become rich from it? Some of the most faithful Christian givers I know are living on fixed incomes and struggle just to get by month by month. Paul meant that, when we are generous in our giving, great spiritual rewards come to us and, not to us only, but to others as well. For example, if we sow sparingly, then our harvest will be sparse. If, however, we give generously, then unimaginable things can be accomplished. Our harvest will be bountiful. Fix in your mind an image of the spiritual harvest which might be reaped as a result of your generous giving. It is staggering to think about.

There was a minister who went to the president of a community bank and inquired about the number of persons in his congregation who made $20,000 or more each year. After receiving the number, he tallied up how much revenue the church would receive if every person tithed 10 percent of his or her earnings. The amount was staggering. On the next Sunday, he told the congregation what he had done and shared with them the results of his study. He described in great detail what things could be done if the church's receipts reflected a title of the church's constituency—things like increasing their mission expenditures, starting a new church across town which they'd been dreaming about for several months, adding a new minister to the church staff, and fixing things that needed repair. Many caught the minister's vision.

Giving generously will bring spiritual rewards limited only by your imagination. Giving in order to receive something in return limits the work of God beyond imagination.

If some give in order to receive, then others give because they are afraid not to. They are afraid of what God might do to them, or someone they love, if they do not give. So their giving serves as a kind of insurance policy against the day of trouble or as protection money against the judgement of God.

Ken Chafin once told of his experience in New Mexico. He came to a little community and a Mexican boy approached him and said, "Hey Mister, I'll watch your car for one American dollar!"

"But the car is right here in the middle of the market," Chafin objected. "What could possibly happen to it?"

The little Mexican cautioned, "Oh, I don't know but somebody might put sand in your gas tank!" Chafin said he felt like he was looking at the "somebody" who would put sand in his tank if he didn't give him a dollar. So Chafin handed him one American dollar as protection money.[1] Some people give protection money to God. Fear is not a healthy motive for giving. Besides, even regular tithers have bad things happen to them in life. There's no such thing as an insurance policy which can be purchased with your tithe.

Some give in order to receive, others give because they are afraid not to and still others give out of a sense of duty or obligation. Look at verses 5 and 7. The Corinthians had promised to give Paul an offering for the saints in Jerusalem. Paul had bragged on the generosity of the Corinthians to the Macedonians much like he had bragged on the Macedonians to the Corinthians and so on (see 8:14). Here, however, Paul wants to make sure his boasting is not in vain. What he says is that, while he was with them, they were eager to give. Now that some time has elapsed since his visit, he wonders if they are still eagerly willing to give or if their willingness has turned into a begrudging obligation.

Some people give because they think they have to. On occasion, you might wonder why in he world you ever agreed to tithe. You still give, but all the joy is gone. You feel like the man who was nominated as a deacon. After being interviewed, the deacon chairman said to him, "Now if you become a deacon, you will have to tithe. Every deacon is to tithe to the regular budget of the church."

His excitement about being nominated turned sour as he murmured, "Well, I guess if I have to, I will!"

Imagine the "fun" he'll have writing his weekly check. Some people give out of a sense of duty or obligation. We should remind such persons, however, "God loves a cheerful giver" (see 9:7). The word translated *cheerful* is the Greek word *hilaron*. If is our word *hilarious*. If someone were to look over your shoulder as you give, would they be apt to say, "Now there's a happy Christian"?

Why Should We Give?

What are the proper motives for giving? What are some healthy reasons why we should give? Paul identifies some of these in this passage.

One of the first reasons why we should give is because it is an extension of our Christian witness. To say we love Christ but do not support the work of His church is about as incongruous as the person who says "I love to golf," but never invests in a set of clubs. Observe what Paul says in verse 10. "Now may He who supplies seed to the sower, and bread for food, supply and multiply the seed you have sown and increase the fruits of your righteousness."

What monetary seed have you sown lately? How is it increasing and producing spiritual benefits? Faithful giving makes the church's mission achieveable, both here and abroad. Most Christians will never be missionaries by profession. However, we are missionaries by practice, even if we are not by profession.

Our witness through giving not only carries out the mission of Christ's church, but it serves to motivate others. Look at the words of Paul in verse 2. "Your zeal has stirred up the majority." What a statement! To think, when I am faithful in my giving, I am helping motivate others to do the same which is an inspiring thought. People who give generously could testify that they learned about tithing from listening and watching those who tithe. Their motivation to tithe came from without long before it came from within.

People and projects depend upon us. That's a second reason why we should give. Paul says that the gifts of the Corinthians help supply the needs of the saints (v. 12). The salaries of career ministers depend on the faithfulness of Christian people. In fact, the entire church program itemized on a church budget is dependent upon the faithfulness of God's people. I don't know who it was that dreamed up the idea of the unified budget. Even with its shortcomings, it's the best system available for facilitating the mission of Christ through the church. Now, you may not agree with every item on a church budget, but by pooling resources and establishing a budget, the church is able to meet the needs of multiple mission projects.

The final and most important reason why we should give is because giving is an act of worship. Look at verse 12: "For the administration of this service." The word translated *administration* is the Greek word *leitourgia*. We derive *liturgy* from that word. The word *liturgy* is made up of two other Greek words *laos* meaning people and *ergon* meaning work. Hence, liturgy is the "work of the people." That's what worship is. It is our work. It is what we "do" together that comprises our worship.

Many of us have a distorted view of worship. Worship is considered as an exercise in which the paid professionals engage while everyone else watches like one would do at a theater. Real worship, however, is something in which we all participate.

Everything we do is an act of worship. Our singing, praying, praising, listening, and giving are acts of worship. Sometimes I think we fail to see that giving is an act of worship. However, when we place our offering in the plate, it is important to remember we are symbolically offering ourselves unto Christ and His church.

For years in our church, it was a practice to pass the plate to the entire congregation but not the choir. Choir members would often give their offering envelopes prior to the service. Since I did not feel it was fair to rob them of this act of worship. I suggested we start passing the plate to the choir members. We established a new tradition that continues today.

It is my conviction that, second only to the invitation time, giving is the most important part of the worship service. Therefore, we should guard against the tendency to place our offerings in the plate in a thoughtless fashion. Remember it is an act of worship and what we *do* in worship fashions who we *are* as Christians. Why give? Because it is a demonstration of your Christian witness. It makes the church's mission possible. But, most of all, it is an act of worship. Worship is the energy of our spiritual lives.

8
Through Courage

The Story of David and Goliath

(1 SAMUEL 17; PHILIPPIANS 4:13)

He looked immense standing nine-and-a-half feet tall. If he were living today, he'd be the highest paid pro-basketball athlete because he could slam-dunk it flatfooted. His armor gripped him as tight as a tourniquet. Clutching a sword and spear, he looked like a Sherman tank wrapped in human flesh. He wore a sweatband across his forehead made of the skin of a lion's carcass. When he walked, it was as if a miniearthquake were taking place, registering 3.0 on the Richter scale. His voice was like a clap of thunder as he marched to the battlefront and hurled his abuses at the frightened Israelite soldiers. His name? Goliath.

Would you take him on? The fact is, there are Goliath-types in all of life. Sometimes Goliath is a formidable decision, a personal problem, a challenging church budget, an enslaving habit, a debilitating temptation, or a mental anxiety. Such Goliaths stand bullishly before us and dare us to come against them. Our first inclination is to run and hide.

There's one young man, however, who chose not to run from Goliath. His name was David. One day Jesse said to his son, David, "Go check on your brothers. I hear the soldiers are at a standstill." Following the instructions, David proceeded to the front line. He found his brothers and other Israelite soldiers standing around a campfire, paralyzed by fear. Just as he was about to ask why, he learned the reason for their timidity. Goliath charged up to the battle-line firing his .50-caliber submachine gun into the air for special effects and daring anyone to come against him. David watched as his comrades ran in every direction like scared rabbits from a skilled hunter.

When the dust cleared, however, David asked, "Who is this muscle-mouth?"

"None like him," replied his frightened brothers. "He's awesome in the worst sense of the word!"

"Nonsense," said David. "The bigger fall harder! So, what's in it for the one who takes him out?"

Sensing his younger brother was entertaining grandiose ideas of taking on Goliath, Eliab said, "David, you're out of your mind. Don't you get any crazy ideas like trying to whip Goliath!"

As did the elder sister in the story of Cinderella, Eliab tries fruitlessly to discourage David. There are always people around like Eliab. Their words are disheartening. Their message is always the same: "You can't do it!" "You'll never pass the exam and qualify for medical school!" "Your marriage won't work!" "You might as well give up!"

Some people seem to hold membership in the "WWCDI Society"—the "Won't-Work-Can't-Do-It Society." Fortunately, however, there are some like David who know that the place of our greatest weakness may also be the place of our greatest strength.

There's a true story about a beggar who wandered into church in a Southern community seeking work.

"It just so happens," said the minister, "there is some work to be done around here." The minister offered him a job on a three-day trial basis. The beggar accepted the offer.

When the days had passed, the beggar came into the office to receive his pay. The minister said, "You've done an exceptional job. Would you like to work here permanently?"

"Sure!" he replied.

"Good!" replied the minister. "Take these employment papers, read them carefully, sign the bottom line, and you've got a job!"

The beggar dropped his head in disappointment.

"What's the matter?" asked the minister. "Did I say something which offended you?"

"No," replied the beggar. "But, you see," he explained, "I can't read or write."

"Oh, really?" asked the minister, astonished. "If you can't read or write, perhaps we should hire someone else for the job."

Leaving the church premises, the beggar cashed his check, bought a variety of fruits and vegetables, and then opened up a fruit stand on the shoulder of a busy roadway.

With the profits from his fruit sale, he bought more fruits and vegetables. When those were sold, he bought still more. Before long, his business was booming.

In just a few short years, he had the largest fruit and vegetable market in the entire region. He purchased land, constructed a warehouse, and in time he made over a million dollars.

One day he went into the local bank where, by this time, he was not only well-known but greatly respected for his entrepreneurship.

Greeting him on a first-name basis, the bank president asked, "How can we be of service to you, Sir?"

"I'd like to open up an account," he said.

The banker escorted him into his office, handed him some account papers, and asked him to fill them out.

The man dropped his head with embarrassment, explaining, "I can't read or write."

"Can't read or write?" the astonished banker asked. "You mean to tell me that you have acquired a financial fortune and you can't read or write?"

"That's right," said the former beggar.

"Incredible!" shouted the banker. "With such business acumen as you obviously possess, do you have any idea where you would be if you could read and write?"

"Yes," replied the man. "I'd be the custodian at the local church."

Sometimes, the place of our weakness is the place of our greatest strength. David knew that. And, it was that knowledge which catapulted David to the front line of the battlefield with a courageous spirit.

"You're but a youth," observed King Saul. "And, furthermore,

Goliath has been a warrior since the day of his youth. What chance could you possibly have against him?" David, however, displayed courage which the apostle Paul declared to the Philippians, "I can do all things through Christ who strengthens me" (Phil. 4:13).

Confidence

David believed in himself. "Thanks for your advice," said David, "but, perhaps, you have not looked closely at my resume. Pretty impressive! Granted, watching sheep on a hillside may not have formed callouses on my hands; but, let me remind you, these hands of mine have caught a lion by its beard and made mincemeat of him."

Confidence in yourself is the first key to confronting your Goliath. You have it within you to meet Goliath. But, you must believe in yourself. Don't let anyone tell you otherwise.

There's a story about a rookie reporter whose great ambition in life was to anchor the evening news. For most of his career, however, he was given the job of a roving reporter. One night, just minutes before the broadcast of the evening news, the usual anchorperson became ill. The news director approached the rookie reporter, saying, "I know you've always wanted to anchor the evening news. Well, it looks as if you'll have that opportunity tonight." The reporter was ecstatic. He started gathering news stories when, minutes before airtime, a news story came across the Associated Press. "The Prime Minister of Afghanistan, Abdul Samalihaikai Begin, had just been assassinated."

Quickly scanning the story, he gasped at the thought of trying to properly pronounce the name for the prime minister.

What will I do? he thought to himself. *I'll never be able to pronounce his name correctly. I'll surely make a fool of myself!*

When the evening broadcast began, however, he had found a way through his dilemma. "Good evening, ladies and gentlemen," he said, "the top news story for the night is this—the prime minister of Afghanistan has been assassinated. His name's being withheld, however, pending notification of the next of kin."

When Goliath, whomever he is or whatever it is, confronts you, believe in yourself. You may be the only one who will.

Resources

David not only believed in himself, but he was well acquainted with his own abilities and resources. That's the second secret to confronting Goliath. Know yourself and your innate abilities and resources. "OK," said King Saul, "if you insist, you've got the job. But, permit me to suggest that you put on my armor, wear my helmet, and wield my sword. If you're to take on Goliath, you've got to look as awesome as Goliath!" David complied. Dashing into the dressing room, he tried on the armor. When he surveyed himself in the mirror, however, he looked as ridiculous as a toddler trying to wear his father's three-piece suit. In addition, it was so heavy he could scarcely move.

"If it's all right with you," said David, "I think I'll use my own weapons."

"And, what are they?" asked the king.

"A sling!" said David.

"A what?" asked the startled man.

"A sling," David replied.

Wagging his head in utter dismay, the king shouted, "You might as well throw snowballs at the Rock of Gilbraltar!"

David knew his own abilities, however. And, he knew that the things which appear the most ridiculous may, in fact, make the most sense.

There was a taxi driver whose cab a passenger climbed in one afternoon. Racing down the street, the driver approached a red light at a busy intersection. Rather than slowing down to stop, however, the driver mashed down on the accelerator and ran the red light. The frantic passenger shouted, "Do you realize you just ran a red light?"

"Yep!" remarked the cabbie, nonchalantly.

"But why?" asked the perplexed passenger.

"My brother always does it," explained the driver. Before long, they came to another red light, and again, the driver raced through the intersection without ever stopping.

"You did it again!" shouted the passenger. "But why?"

"My brother always does it," the driver responded.

After running several red lights, the taxi approached another intersection where the light was green. This time, however, the cabbie slammed on his brakes and came to a screeching halt.

"The light's green," observed the passenger. "You're supposed to go on."

"Can't do it!" responded the cabbie, while looking at him through his rearview mirror.

"But why?" asked the astonished passenger.

"Because," he explained, "You never know when my brother may be coming!"

Sometimes, the most sensible things are those which appear as the most ridiculous. David knew that, just as did the taxi driver.

Here is a simple formula for facing your Goliath. You, plus God, equals everything you'll ever need. That's not to say you'll have everything you want. But, when you take you abilities and combine them with God's availability, there's not Goliath anywhere who is able to destroy you. Granted, Goliath may inflict a few wounds, but he will never ultimately wipe you out.

A little boy, whose left arm had been severed in an accident, came to Sunday School. Hoping to avoid making him feel conspicuous, the teacher decided not to do anything which required the children to use both of their hands. The class went smoothly until the end of the hour. Forgetting, momentarily, what she had decided earlier, the teacher closed the class period with her usual exercise. "All right now, children, before we leave today, let's build our church together!" She proceeded to lead them in the finger play, "Here's the church, here's the steeple; Open the doors, and see the people."

No sooner than she began, however, that the error of her ways dawned upon her. Frozen with embarrassment, she wondered what to do for the one-armed child. To her rescue came a little girl beside whom the one-armed boy sat. She said, "Here take my left hand and let's build the church together."

In many ways, God is like that little girl. When Goliath stands mockingly before us, God comes to us, saying, "Take your abilities in one hand, and in the other, take My hand, and together, let's meet Goliath courageously!"

Trust

There's one other thing David did which empowered him to face Goliath. He trusted God completely. "Moreover," said David, "the Lord who delivered me from the paw of the bear and lion will deliver me today!" (see v. 37). Is this not what the apostle Paul said under different but, similar, circumstances? "I can do all things through Christ who strengthens me!" (Phil. 4:13). Paul did not say, "I can do all things," but "I can do all things through Christ." Christ is the means by which we face our Goliaths fearlessly.

When we trust in God, our perspective on things suddenly changes. Our Goliaths are reduced in size, making them more manageable and, sometimes, even defeatable. That is not to say Goliath will always be defeated in this life. When we know who is on our side, however, Goliath will never be bigger than our ability to manage.

Whenever I think of our changing perspective, I think about the story in which a young coed had written a letter to her parents after completing a semester of studies in college. As nearly as I can recall, the letter went something like this:

Dear Mom and Dad,
Just thought I'd drop you a note and clue you in on my plans. I've fallen in love with a guy called Jim. He quit high school after the eleventh grade in order to get married. About a year ago, he got a divorce. We've been going together almost two months and plan to get married in the fall. Until then, I've decided to move into his apartment, because I think I might be pregnant. At any rate, I dropped out of school last week, although I'd like to finish college sometime in the future.

Can you imagine how those parents felt after receiving such a letter? They must have been shocked. Fortunately, however, there was more written on the back side of the letter. It read as follows:

Dear Mom and Dad,
I just want you to know that everything I've written on the front side
of this letter is false. But, this much is true. I got a C— in French, and I
flunked math. It's also true, I need more money for tuition payments.
Love, your daughter.

After reading the back side of the letter, you can imagine what
the parents were probably singing, "Oh, what a relief it is!" What
was the difference between the front side and the back side of the
letter? Perspective! That's all!

Think about David's experiences. While David's brothers were
looking at Goliath and feeling afraid, David was looking at God and
feeling courageous. If you think about it, the underdog in the story
is not David at all, but Goliath. It is not David coming against Goliath, but Goliath coming against God. I saw a bumper sticker once
which read, "How big is your God?" Good questions! How big is
He? Is He big enough to help you confront the Goliaths of your life?
Is He big enough to help you deal with your marriage which may be
on the rocks? What about that vigorous work schedule under which
you live? Or that new responsibility to which you have pledged
yourself? Is your God big enough? You bet He is. Because the question is not how big God is but how big your faith is? Jesus said that
faith, the size of a mustard seed, is big enough (Matt. 17:20). That's
all it takes. So, go for it! Your Goliath has no idea what he's up
against.

9
Through Worship
Permitting Christ to Meet Your Deepest Need

(MARK 2:1-12)

The service was in progress. The house was full just the way most ministers like it. The guest speaker was Jesus Himself who stood to His feet and started His sermon. No sooner had He made the first point, however, when everyone's attention was riveted to the ceiling as the noise of footsteps made it seem as if the roof itself would fall on them. Indeed, to their astonishment, a portion of the roof was removed, and as the people below rubbed their eyes of the dusty debris and plucked the fallen pieces of plaster from their hair, they heard one of the nameless intruders say, "Yep, here He is! Let's lower the stretcher right here!"

The crowd was stunned. In silence, they watched as four men lowered a fifth man to the feet of Jesus. "Son, your sins are forgiven you." "Arise, take up your bed and walk." These words were among the things Jesus said to the helpless man. Within moments, the paralyzed man stood to his feet, folded his pallet, and walked out of the crowded house. The astonished worshipers ended their stunned silence by saying, "We never saw anything like this" (v. 12.)

I understand their astonishment. There are times I come to worship and long for something out of the ordinary to happen. My life, including my worship, all too frequently becomes mundane and predictable.

I am reminded of the story told of a little boy who went to live with his grandmother. She was a very devout Christian whose loyalty to her church prohibited her from ever missing a service.

One day the circus came to their community. That would not

have been so unusual except that, in this case, the circus was to perform only once, and the performance was to take place during prayer meeting on Wednesday night.

"May I go to the circus?" pleaded the boy.

"Of course not!" replied Grandma. "You know that we always go to prayer meeting on Wednesday night."

"I know, Grandma," he continued. "But there's only one performance. May I go just this once? Please? Please?"

Against her better wishes, she consented. "Just this once, but never again!" she instructed.

Later that evening when the boy had returned from the circus and Grandma had returned from church, she asked him, "Well, how did it go?"

He thought for a moment and then confessed, "Well, Grandma, if you ever go to the circus once, you'll never want to go back to prayer meeting on Wednesday night!"

Do you ever feel that way about worship? The story of the healing of the paralytic reminds us of how the mundaneness of our life and worship may be interrupted and redeemed by Christ. Take a fresh look at this story with me. Who knows how your life may be "surprised by joy," as C. S. Lewis put it.

There are several interesting things about this episode in the life and ministry of Jesus. One is the characters around whom the drama unfolds. You will observe the crowd of people packed tightly in the house, some of whom were friendly toward Jesus, while others were unfriendly—namely the scribes (v. 6).

There is the paralytic himself—helpless and hopeless—in whom Jesus performs a miracle of healing. And then, there are the four philanthropists—committed, compassionate, and creative in their efforts at bringing the paralyzed man to Jesus. Any one of these characters or groups of persons—the people, paralytic, or philanthropists—invites careful study.

Before we examine the characters of the story and what each may mean to us, however, take a look at the conversations which took place. You will notice that much of the dialogue is below the surface, so to speak. For example, the philanthropists never say a word but Jesus looks into their hearts and responds to their faith (v. 5).

The crowd of people in the story say nothing until the end; amazed at the healing of the paralytic, they glorify God saying, "We have never seen anything like this" (v. 12). The scribes do speak but not aloud. They complain in their hearts, and Jesus carries on a dialogue with their nonverbal complaints (vv. 6-8). If you think about it, all of the characters and conversations are important to the interpretation and application of the story to our lives. Given that fact, the most significant conversation is the one between Jesus and the paralytic. Again, you will notice the conversation takes place beneath the surface of consciousness. Jesus looked beyond the paralytic's most obvious need—the need for physical healing—and speaks to the paralytic's greatest need—the need for spiritual healing. "My son," said Jesus, "your sins are forgiven" (v. 5, RSV).

Both the characters in the story and their conversations with Jesus remind me of how often each of us comes to church, and on the surface, we look as if we have it all together but deep down we have needs—needs which may not be so apparent to the casual observer but needs which Christ alone can meet.

To me the whole point of the miracle story is that each of us must let Christ meet our deepest needs and those needs are represented in the three groups of persons found in the story—the paralytic, philanthropists, and people.

The Paralytic: Our Unspoken Needs

There's a sense in which each of us is like the paralytic. We have needs which we may never share with anyone else, but they are nonetheless real.

In the church where I serve, we have a place in our order of worship where we stop everything, look together at a prayer list on which the names of those hospitalized, homebound, and in nursing homes are printed, and then we pray together for those persons and their needs. I never lead the gathered congregation in the pastoral prayer without reminding myself that all of those under the sound of my voice have needs and burdens, too. The truth is, I have needs of my own, and while no one present may know of those needs, they are real to me.

In the story, the paralytic represents each of us and our unspoken needs—needs which may be unknown to others, but at the same time, known and understood by Christ.

What do you feel you need right now more than anything else? Sometimes, I think we become a little mixed up about this. For example, there are times we feel what we need is to "fit in" with our peers at school or colleagues at work, when perhaps what we really need is to learn to enjoy our acceptance to Christ. I counseled a couple once whose marriage was anything but ideal. They decided what their lives needed was to build a new house in a new neighborhood. I felt, however, what they really needed was to discover the meaning of love and start construction on a home not a house.

There are times we're tempted to feel that a more prestigious degree or larger place of service will give us the recognition we deserve when what we really need is the recognition of Christ and the rediscovery of purpose where we are.

The fashion craze of our culture and the crass materialism of our society often blinds us to our real needs. We try to bolster our image by changing our wardrobe. We seek happiness in the fruitless pursuit of things. I think it would help all of us recognize our deeper need to have our values changed by Christ and learn the secret of contentment borne out of a relationship to Christ. Mother Teresa rightly said that you will never know Jesus is all you need until Jesus is all you got. It takes far too long for many of us to learn that simple but profound truth.

I do not know if the paralytic was aware of his unspoken need for forgiveness. The philanthropists who brought him to Jesus were obviously unaware of any need beyond that of physical healing. I do believe, however, that Jesus knows you and me better than we know ourselves, and He has not only the willingness but the power to meet our unspoken needs. Will you permit Him to meet yours? The secret of true worship lies in the acknowledgment of our individual needs. Out-of-the-ordinary things happen in worship with this fundamental acknowledgment.

The Philanthropists: Our Need to Be Useful

My imagination is captured by these four nameless fellows. When I read this story, I imagine what might happen should one of our worship services be interrupted by latecomers bringing people to Christ from all over the community that our church serves. There are two things which frighten me about such a thought. One is that some church members would be upset because worship was interrupted. The other is that it is hard to imagine such an occurrence because, the truth is, we so seldom bring people to Christ. Perhaps this is why these four men are so compelling to me. They represent the mission of the church and our need to be useful to God in carrying out that mission.

In his book *Your Other Vocation*, Elton Trueblood said, "Unless we can go to work with God on Monday we are not likely, in the long run, to have any effective worship of God on Sunday, and if we do engage in the latter, it becomes a sham."[1]

The four men are remarkable in many ways. For one thing, they are cooperative in their efforts. What they accomplished cooperatively would have been impossible individually. Fulfilling the mission of the church—which is bringing people to Jesus—is possible when we are united in our efforts.

Their compassion is commendable. In a world where it was easy not to care about anything or anyone, here was a group of persons who were motivated by love.

They were also creative in their techniques. If I had been one of the four fellows, I would have probably given up at the crowded door and suggested to the others that we return the paralytic to his home.

The most remarkable thing about these four men, however, was the conviction of their hearts. They were convinced that Jesus could make a difference in the paralytic's life if they could only succeed in bringing him to Christ.

When Jesus looked up at these four men as they lowered their friend to His feet, what do you think Jesus admired most about them? Their cooperation? Their compassion? Their creativity? Perhaps! But, I think what most impressed Him was their belief in His power to change life dramatically. The Bible says, "When Jesus saw their faith" (v. 5), He was moved to help the paralytic. It was their faith in Christ and the difference He could make in their friend's life which impressed Jesus.

Sometimes, I think it is important for us to ask ourselves what we believe Jesus can do for the people we bring to Him. What do you believe? What difference can He make in the lives of those with whom you work? Can Christ do anything for your neighbor next door? Are you allowing Him to make a difference in your own life? If there's anything the church needs today, it is a renewal of belief in the power of Christ to change human life. And, if there's anything each individual believer needs, it is fresh commitment to the church's mission of bringing people to Jesus. You have a need to be useful. The mission of the church can meet your need. And, it goes without saying, your enjoyment of worship is unmistakably tied to your involvement is the church's mission. Worship without witness is contradictory.

The People: Our Deepest Need

The crowd that gathered around Jesus was made up of two principal groups of people—those friendly toward Him and those troubled by Him. The scribes were hostile toward Jesus. The rest were friendly toward Him or simply curious about Him. There is one thing, however, they all, whether hostile or friendly, shared in common. What do you suppose was that common denominator they all shared?

Let me ask it another way. Why do you suppose people come to church today? There are perhaps many reasons, but I can think of a few of the more common ones. For a few people, there is no other place to be on Sunday but with God's people in worship. Their love of Christ constrains them to gather with God's people to celebrate the resurrection of the Lord. They long for it and look forward to it.

For others coming to church is a matter of responsibility. They live with a tremendous sense of "oughtness" about church attendance. Having made a commitment to Christ and His church, they feel obligated to attend whether they like it or experience much from it.

Since many of us are creatures of habit, I am sure there are some who come as a matter of habit. It's part of their normal routine like getting up daily and going to work. There may be little thought or preparation about it. They're so accustomed to coming that little, if any, investment is necessary.

It is hardly conceivable but humanly possible that a few come to keep from tarnishing an image or jeopardizing a social standing in the community. It is difficult for me to imagine this as a conscious motivation, but I am certain it must unconsciously motivate some persons to come to church.

These are perhaps only a few of the many reasons why people come to church but, I believe, beneath and behind all the possible motivations is the primary motivation—each of us longs to find God or, better still, be found by Him. The truth is, our deepest need is to know God personally. The "something unusual" we long for in worship is Someone whom we call God.

Last Thanksgiving Day, we went to Springfield, Kentucky, to celebrate the holiday with my wife's family. On the way, I decided I would not spend the day, as in the past, watching the Macy's Parade on television in the morning, gorging myself on turkey and dressing at lunch, and then passively watching the football games in the afternoon. Rather, I made up my mind to spend most of the day playing outside with my children and their cousins. As it turned out, it was one of the better decisions I've made lately.

We had loads of fun. We played sword fight with some plastic baseball bats, and when they grew old, we played cops and robbers with toys my wife Marsha and her brother Jimmy had as children. We threw a Frisbee and placed soccer in the wide-open field next door to Granddaddy and Mammaw Mann's house. We even had a little funeral service for a squirrel and a bird the children found dead in the field.

I look back on that Thanksgiving Day with more fondness than I can describe on paper. The image which has brazened itself upon my mind is what I observed while we played a game of "Kick-the-Can." You know how the game goes. Like "Hide-and-Seek" all participants run and hide while the person who's "it" stands beside an empty can and counts to fifty. Then, the one who's "it" goes in search of those who've hidden, and when he or she finds you or sees you, the two of you race back to home base. If the one who's "it" reaches the can first, then you're "it." If, however, you get back first, then you kick the can as far as you can, which makes it possible for everyone else to run back to home base whereupon the whole process is started over.

I noticed an interesting thing as we played. Every time I was "it" the kids would always hide so they'd be sure I'd have no trouble finding them. If it appeared I was about to run past where they were hiding, they would giggle or clear their throats to make sure I would find them. I kept thinking to myself, *Why do they want me to find them so quickly and effortlessly?* It was a perplexing thought until I remembered the story in Mark's Gospel and the reason why people come to church. The real reason people come to church is no different than that of the kids playing "Kick-the-Can" with me. The children wanted me to find them just as each of us wants God to find us. There is no greater need which any of us have than the need to be found by God. And the message of this story is that our need to be found by the Father is met in Jesus Christ. Has He found you, yet?

10
Through Intimacy

Home Is Where You Hang Your Hat (or Is It Heart?)

(PSALM 127)

The end is intimacy. The means is the home. Yet, in this highly impersonal world, the first place where intimacy is born and nurtured is often the last place where it is found and experienced. We frequently find ourselves in the dilemma one family did while traveling on vacation. The father was driving while his wife, two children, and dog rode in the trailer attached to the car.

A state trooper signaled to him to pull over onto the shoulder of the highway. The officer informed him that one of his taillights was out. The driver broke out in a cold sweat, and the trooper consoled him by saying he was not going to give him a ticket.

"That's not why I'm upset," said the driver, "but if you can see my taillights, that means I've lost a trailer, a wife, two kids, and a dog."

All too frequently, families find themselves in trouble because too little attention is given in the home. Then, when a crisis erupts, couples seek a marriage counselor and want to change twenty years of a poor marriage in a few counseling sessions. Stretching a bandage across that which requires major surgery, however, will never work.

Elton Trueblood once wrote: "The individual home may seem a tiny thing in comparison to states and governments and armies, but it is by means of such tiny things that the world is changed . . . . If we could have enough good homes, we should have a very different world."[1].

The same logic applies to the church. If we could have enough good homes, we should have a very different church. The church must provide help for the home.

There is a lovely and instructive psalm which relates to the home. Psalm 127 is one of two psalms whose authorship is attributed to Solomon. The basic premise of Somomon's psalm is this: All our human endeavors in life are vain without absolute trust in God. That is to say, if we are to build homes (the place where you hang your heart) and not simply houses (the place where you hang your hat), we must begin with complete trust in what God says about the institution He founded.

What does this psalm tell us about the home?

The Foundation of the Home

Solomon observes, "Unless the Lord builds the house, They labor in vain who build it" (v. 1).

When Solomon said, "Unless the Lord builds the house," he was reminding us of the importance of building our homes upon the proper foundation. What is the proper foundation for the home? It is spiritual in nature. When couples decide to be married, they need to believe that God has blessed their consummation in marriage. One of the first questions I ask a couple who comes to me for premarital counseling is, "Why do you want to get married?" The answer I look for is the one which reflects their conviction that God Himself is pleased with their marriage plans. When their answers do not reflect that conviction, I try to spend time exploring with them the importance of having such a conviction.

Several years ago, a couple approached me about performing their marriage ceremony. I agreed, and we met several times to talk about marriage and plan for their wedding.

Two weeks to the day after the wedding, I received a letter from the bride drenched with hostility. In it, she said, "My husband and I were shocked when you read Scripture and said a prayer in our wedding ceremony. Who gave you permission to do that?" On and on she went expressing her disappointment and anger toward me for my making reference to anything spiritual in their wedding ceremony.

To say the least, I was grieved by her letter. After thinking about what I should do, I sat down one afternoon and wrote a response to them. It went something like this:

> Dear Bill and Martha, I am grieved to know you feel as you do about the wedding ceremony I performed for you. What grieves me most is that you have begun your marriage with such an unhappy memory of what should be the happiest memory of your married life—your wedding day. If I have understood your letter correctly, what has angered you most is my use of scripture and prayer in your ceremony. Let me remind you, however, that I am a Christian minister. I believe in prayer. I believe in the Bible. And, I believe what the Bible says about marriage is right and worthy of our attention and respect. Because of that, I did not feel I needed anyone's permission to use Scripture and prayer in your ceremony. If you had wanted a service devoid of Scripture and prayer, perhaps you should have requested the services of a Justice of the Peace.

I never heard from them after sending the letter. But, I have learned one thing, and that is to talk forthrightly to couples about their relationship to God, the kind of foundation upon which they plan to build their home, and the place of worship in both their ceremony and married life.

Upon what foundation is your home being built? Marriage counselors talk a lot about building the home on a strong relational foundation. So do I. It is important that couples learn how to communicate, share similar interests and hobbies, fight fairly, disagree agreeably, and be intimate and caring toward each other. I think the first place to begin is with their spiritual relationship. How does God figure into the marriage? What does He mean to you personally? What place does worship hold in your relationship? And, will your wedding service be simply a ceremony or a celebration of worship?

The Securities for the Home

The second observation Solomon made is as salient as the first. "Unless the Lord guards the city, The watchman stays awake in vain" (v. 1).

Solomon's inspiration for these words must surely have come from his observation of the watchmen who were stationed strategically along the walls of Jerusalem as guards over the city (Isa. 62:6). For the inhabitants within the city walls, a sense of security developed as they trusted the watchmen to remain alert and notify them in the event of an approaching invader. Contemplating it, however, Solomon seemed to feel that, in spite of the noble attempts of the guards to protect the city against harm, disasters struck nonetheless in the forms of famines, plagues, and disease. Enemies, interestingly, invaded their ranks not from without but from within the city walls.

The greatest enemies of the home today are within the home. Jesus said, "A man's foes will be those of his own household," (Matt. 10:36). In the Song of Solomon, the writer reminds us that it is "The little foxes that spoil the vines" (2:15). Insensitivity, infidelity, and misplaced priorities are a few of the contemporary invaders of the home. These enemies have left far too many casualties on the battlefields of divorce courts.

Therefore, the home needs something with which to make it secure. What are the securities of the home? One security for your home is your relationship to God. If the home can be compared to an athletic team, then families need to know that God is a team member. They need to believe that God wants them to not only score a touchdown but win decisively. Make Christ and His church the center of your family life. However, don't make the mistake one man whom I know made. Bob became so involved in doing church work, teaching Sunday School, serving as an elder, and working with committees that, before long, he was at church more than he was at home. He realized his mistake the day his wife asked for a divorce. Today, Bob lives alone and, unfortunately, blames the church for his error in judgment.

A second security for the family is other families. Every family needs two or three other families with whom to share experiences and depend on in times of difficulty and stress. Families whom you can get together for a cookout, go camping with over the weekend, and pray with. The day may come when you need some friends.

Learning how to play together as families is a third security for the home. Eric Byrne, the father of transactional analysis, used to say that the truly healthy person is one who can say, "Yes, No, and Whoopee!" What is true of the healthy person is true of the healthy family. Families must learn to cast off the restraints on time associated with responsibilities long enough to engage in a little "Whoopee!"

The element of surprise is a security for the home. A few years ago, Neil Diamond sang a song entitled "You Don't Bring Me Flowers Anymore!" My first reaction after hearing it was "Well, why not?" The most exciting marriages are those wherein the element of surprise is nurtured.

Other securities for the home are communication, education, and family devotions. Learn to talk openly and honestly with each other about everything—your family life, work life, social life, church life, sex life, and so forth.

Take advantage of educational opportunities your church or community may provide in the way of marriage enrichment retreats and family life weekends.

Above all, have a family devotion time. Use the method of storytelling. I think it is more effective than reading selections of Scripture at the supper table or buying a video of the story of Noah's ark and sitting your children down in front of the television set. If your children are like mine, they spend far too much time setting like zombies in front of the TV, anyway. Learn the great stories of our faith and tell them in simple but creative ways to your children. You'll probably find your children, as I have mine, will rarely retire for the evening without requesting to hear a Bible story. I know I have told the story of the prodigal son at least one hundred times. Yet, it never fails, when I get to the part about the son's grand homecoming, we all feel a little closer, more in love, and more secure as a family ourselves.

The Pace of the Home

Solomon continues, "It is vain for you to rise up early, To sit up late, To eat the bread of sorrows; For so He gives His beloved sleep" (v. 2).

These words show concern about the primary focus of one's life—the ambition, goal, or purpose of your life which gets you up in the morning and motivates you even during the late hours of the night. *The Jerusalem Bible* provides a translation of this verse that is insightful. "In vain you get up earlier, and put off going to bed, sweating to make a living."

"Sweating to make a living." Ah, that's our problem, isn't it? When the sole ambition of life is to "make a living," it is hard not to keep from getting up earlier and staying up later.

Maturity is acting your age instead of your urge," said a wise person. What is your primary urge? Making money? Climbing to the top of the Wall Street ladder? Tracking the Stock Exchange? Seeing your name in print? None of these are unworthy ambitions. What about being the best Christian parent you can be? Or, what about the amount of time you spend with your spouse? Notice, I use the words "amount of time." A few years ago, family counselors argued in favor of quality time not the quantity of time. They successfully convinced us that the kind of time we spend with our family is more important than the amount of time we are together. In principle, they are right. However, I have the feeling their advice merely gave the ambitious working parent an excuse for being an absentee landlord. What is needed today, however, is enough time to nurture the quality kind of family relationships we need to have strong, secure homes. As you schedule your daily business appointments, schedule time for your spouse and family. Keep the appointments with your family with as much conscientiousness and presence as you do other appointments. And don't forget to take care of yourself. Make the right choice with regard to yourself and your family. It is yours to make.

The Value We Place on Parenting

There is a final instructive point Solomon makes in this psalm.

"Behold, children are a heritage from the Lord.
The fruit of the womb is His reward.
Like arrows in the hand of a warrior,

So are the children of one's youth.
Happy is the man who has his quiver full of them;
They shall not be ashamed.
But shall speak with their enemies in the gate (vv. 3-5).

For Hebrew families, the highest priority was placed on children. Apart from the economic necessities which motivated their desires to have large families, children were the means by which Hebrew parents experienced some measure of immortality. They lived on by living through their children.

Solomon observes, "Happy is the man who has his quiver full of them." The image he uses is interesting. A *quiver* was a pouch used by a soldier to carry his arrows. The more arrows a soldier had in his quiver, the better prepared he was to wage battle. The point Solomon is making is simply that having children is a valuable enterprise and better prepares one for life.

As you well know, times have changed. Whether you have a quiver full of them or only one in each hand, the responsibilities associated with parenting are the same in every age. If God has blessed you with children, you are blessed indeed. Few things are more painful to a married couple than the desire to have children but the inability, for whatever reason, to have them.

If you have been so blessed, however, your responsibility is to rear those children yourself. What I fear today is that the privilege of rearing children is being turned over increasingly to day-care centers and baby-sitters. What children need more than anything else is a parent who is available. Availability breeds intimacy and is manifested by listening, loving, and laughing together.

The manufacturers of a baby-products company have a TV commercial picturing a mother caressing her baby. The announcer observes, "Touch, the language of love." Take time to touch your children. Play ball with them and experience some of their contagious laughter and innocence. Turn off the television long enough to read a story to them.

Just two nights ago, I walked outside to meditate on the Scripture story from which I was fashioning my Sunday sermon. My attention was rivited, however, to the harvest moon, so bright and large that I felt as if I could reach out and touch it. The sky was crystal clear, not a cloud in sight to hide the countless glistening stars which appeared as diamonds on a black velvet canvas. For a moment, I was lost in the magnificence of it all, when my son stuck his head out the front door of our house wondering where I was and calling out to me. "Daddy," he cried, "where are you?"

"Come quickly," I insisted. "And bring your sister." In minutes, the two of them were standing on either side of me. "Sit down with me, kids. I want you to see something." They obediently sat down, and I nudged them close to me by putting my arms around them. For the next few but precious minutes, I talked with them about the moon and its distance from the earth, recent of the *Discovery* shuttle, vastness of space, bigness of God, and stars which are millions of light years from us. They listened. I explained. They questioned. I struggled for answers, since I'm no astronomer and hardly a precise theologian. It was a rare but real moment of intimacy we shared. And, the realness of that moment which I relish the most is the moment of intimacy in which my children required nothing from me. It required only me. Home is where I hang my heart. And, you know what? It may be the same for you.

11
Through Trust

*Learning to Manage Your
Fear and Anxiety*

(NUMBERS 13:25-33; MATTHEW 6:25-34)

Someone has said, "Worry is fear exposed." It's true. Ours is an anxious, "fear-full" world. A recent survey revealed that nearly half of all U.S. citizens have guns in their homes, and one in every ten persons carries a weapon at all times. The survey reveals just how rampant fear is in our society. Now, some fear is healthy. You should be afraid of your child sticking her finger into an electrical socket. It should cause you to shiver with fear at the prospects of a nuclear exchange between the nations of this world. In most instances, however, our fears and anxieties are unhealthy. They stem from unmet needs, unexamined priorities and ambitions, or an imagination left uncontrolled.

Look at a few of the more common ones. There's the fear of going unrecognized, of not being noticed or accepted. We spend much of our lives auditioning for the approval of others. We are terrified at the prospects of being overlooked.

Recently I was conducting a series of services in a church in western Kentucky. One day, I had lunch with a minister from the area. In the course of our conversation, he told me that at one time he was a minister of music in a large church.

"Oh, you are a singer as well as a preacher?" I asked. "Few of us are so gifted."

"Well," he explained, "I used to be a singer. But, the Lord told me never to sing again."

I was curious, so I said, "I hope you don't mind my questions, but I am perplexed by your comment that God told you to never sing again. Why would God tell you that?"

"Because," he continued, "there was this identity problem some people had with me. When I decided to become a pastor, everyone still expected me to lead the singing. I would go to associational meetings and folks kept calling on me to sing. Nobody recognized me as a preacher. So, God told me to quit singing!"

Ah! I thought to myself. *I think I understand.* The key word in his comment is *recognize*. I'm no psychoanalyst, but it seems to me that in his frustration over his identity as a singer he feared he might go unrecognized as a pastor. Rather than coming to grips with his newly acquired identity as a musician/preacher, he felt one had to be sacrificed at the altar of the other. The sad thing is he blamed it all on God. In our fear of being unrecognized and unaccepted, we often do odd things and concoct awkward explanations for our actions.

The fear of failure is another anxiety with which we live. In my profession as a minister, when church people are offered an opportunity for service in the church, I often hear them respond by saying, "I can't do it," "I'm not sure if I can," or "Perhaps you should find someone else who is more qualified." I wonder if those outward responses reflect an inward fear of failure?

There is the fear of change. Can you believe how rapidly things change? My ninety-year-old grandmother has seen our world's means of transportation change from the horse-drawn buggy to intercontinental travel by jet, not to mention the placing of a man on the moon. I know it sounds absurd, but we're told that one-half of all we know today has been learned in the last twenty-five years.

Think about medical science. I read recently about a woman in Pittsburgh who suffered a cerebral aneurysm. The doctors put her in a comatose state, stopped her heart, chilled her body to forty degrees, drained her body of most of its blood (the condition which, up to this time in medical history would have classified her as clinically dead), and performed surgery by removing the aneurysm. Then, they repumped the blood into her body and started her heart. Today she is living a normal life and calling her remarkable recovery a "cotton-pickin' miracle."[1]

Then, there is the fear of fear itself. Someone has said, "Nothing is so frightening as a bunch of scared people." The ominous threat of a nuclear exchange, for example, is enough to frighten us. I believe in a strong defense. But, when is strong enough? How many conventional or nuclear weapons does it take to make us feel secure? It seems to me that in stockpiling more and more nuclear weapons to make us feel secure we only succeed in producing the exact opposite—the feeling of insecurity. Insecure people are scared people.

Have you ever considered how frequently the words *fear not* appear in the Bible? Those words or some form of those words appear 365 times in Scripture. That's one for every day of the year. God wants us to live free of debilitating fear. Scripture supports the thesis that our anxieties and fears are manageable.

The key word is *manageable*. Fear and anxiety cannot be eradicated entirely. They are a part of the very fabric of life. When the twelve spies returned from checking out the land of Canaan, they were all afraid, including Joshua and Caleb. The story does not tell us ten spies were afraid and only Joshua and Caleb were brave. The fact is they were all terrified by the threats beyond the Jordan. The difference between the majority report (the report of the ten spies) and the minority report (the report of Joshua and Caleb) is found in the confidence of the minority in the promises of God. I think we need to remember that a majority may only mean that the disbelieving are all on the same side. God had promised the land to the Israelites. Joshua and Caleb were willing to stake their lives on that promise, in spite of how they felt. Trusting God does not automatically erase your fears. It does, however, keep your fears and anxieties in perspective (Num. 13:25-33).

Jesus had much to say about the management of our fears. Perhaps His most poignant statement about it is found in the Sermon on the Mount. Jesus was speaking to His followers. Visualize yourself sitting on the mountainside eagerly absorbing His words as He outlines a strategy for managing our fears and anxieties. He offers several suggestions.

The Futility of Excessive Anxiety and Fear

Jesus asks, "Which of you by worrying can add one cubit to his stature?" (v. 27) The word *stature* has been debated by Scripture scholars. The *King James Version* translates the Greek word with *stature* to capture the image of one wishing he could instantly add a cubit (approximately eighteen inches) to his height. I can remember a time when, in grade school, I longed to be taller so that I could better compete in the game of basketball. Did my wishful thinking make me any taller? Of course not!

The *Revised Standard Version*, on the other hand, translates the same Greek word with the words *span of life*, meaning the length of life. If one follows that translation, Jesus was asking, "Which of you can add one cubit to his span of life by worrying?" Will fear and anxiety lengthen one's life? Again, the answer is no! In fact, recent medical studies have indicated that excessive anxiety and fear might even shorten life. Someone has said, "It's not toil but trouble that turns the hair grey before its time." The stress which accompanies unmanaged fear is life-threatening. Isn't it true, as someone has said, "More die of worry than work, because many more worry than work?"

Regardless of which translation you prefer, the principle is the same. Excessive worry will neither increase your height nor lengthen your life. In fact, it is counterproductive and will accomplish nothing. Dr. C. Roy Angell once said, "There was a sad bit of humor in the statement of a young lady the other day when she said, 'I am such a good worrier that I have been thinking of making it a profession and charging people for doing their worrying for them.'"

Someone once asked, "Do you want a nervous breakdown?" Here's a recipe:

Find out what kind of worry suits your temperament and then stick to it. Personally, I like to track down some absurd little frustration, nurse it along, and build it up into a fine upstanding disaster. It appeals to the creative artist in me to mail a letter and then start worrying whether I put a stamp on it or addressed it properly until I am a nervous wreck. Oh, and don't neglect your health as a subject. You may think you are well now, but, chances are you are coming down with something serious this very moment. Let no day pass without crying over spilt milk, even if you have to spill it yourself.

At best, excessive worry is futile. Acknowledge its futility. That's the place to begin in learning to manage fear and anxiety.

The Surrender of Fear and Anxiety

A second strategy Jesus suggests for managing our fears and anxieties is to surrender tomorrow's troubles to tomorrow. He says, "Therefore do not worry about tomorrow, for tomorrow will worry about its own things. Sufficient for the day is its own trouble" (v. 34). Notice Jesus does not advise us to avoid planning for the future. We should plan for tomorrow and make every preparation possible to protect ourselves and our families from the contingent and accidental.

There is a Christian man in a church I once served who learned the hard way the importance of preparing for the uncertainties of the future. Thinking he would never need it, he failed to purchase adequate health insurance coverage for his family and himself. His wife developed cancer, however, and it eventually took her life. Today, he finds himself in one legal battle after another as hospitals sue him for the thousands of dollars he owes in unpaid medical bills that his wife incurred before her death. While we should prepare for the future, we need not fret over the future. "Sufficient for the day is its own trouble" (v. 34). Stated another way, Jesus is saying, "Live in the present. Live one day at a time."

In his book *How to Know When You've Got It Made*, Ken Chafin makes the point that the two worst enemies of living in the present begin with the question "What if . . ." and the statement "If only . . ." The question "What if . . ." turns our imagination loose to explore all the uncertainties of the future. What if I fail in school? What if my friends don't accept me? What if I lose my job? What if I don't pass the exam? What if I have cancer? What if I'm left alone?

On the other hand, the statement "If only . . ." opens the window of our memory to observe the failures of our past. We resurrect our guilt by remembering the wrongs we have done. We ridicule ourselves by recalling what we have left undone. We renew our anger by replaying the tapes of past conversations, conflicts, and hurts. In short, we poison the present by swallowing the pain of the past.[2]

As a child I heard the story of a mother who placed her children inside the fenced-in backyard to play one afternoon. Her adult suspicions got the best of her when she saw her children huddled together. She slipped through the back door and quietly approached her children to see what it was that had captured their attention. Peering over her son's shoulder, she was terrified to see her children watching a mother skunk with her young.

"Run, children, run!" she shouted at the top of her lungs. Startled by her presence but obedient to her command, each child quickly grabbed up a baby skunk and ran toward the house.

We laugh at the prospects of such an occurrence. But, isn't it true that many of us race through life carrying with us the very thing which can ruin the fragrance of our todays? Christ wants us to accept His forgiveness for the past and trust His presence for the future. That's the second strategy for learning to manage our fears and anxieties.

The Freedom of Faith

Faith in God's faithfulness is mandatory for developing the fine art of managing our fears and anxieties. "Is not life more than food and the body more than clothing?" asked Jesus (vv. 25-29) "Look at the birds of the air . . . . Consider the lilies of the field." Jesus was saying that creation has a divinely programmed system for taking care of itself. The fowl of the air do not frantically store food in barns. The Father feeds them. The wild flowers neither toil nor sweat. Yet, their beauty is unsurpassed. Jesus' point is, "If God takes care of the fowl of the air and clothes the fields with flowers, is He not much more likely to take care of you?" Well, is He? Only faith can answer that question. Faith spells freedom just as disbelief spells anxiety.

God wants us to learn to trust ourselves to Him. That does not mean we passively resign ourselves to the inevitable as if everything happens in a predetermined fashion. We are not simply pawns in the hands of an impassionate deity. Nor does the tapestry of our lives unfold in a preprogrammed manner. In a recent article in *Psychology Today* two noted professors, Daniel McIntosh and Bernard Spilka observed, "The way that Christians view their relationship to God may affect their health. The view that 'God helps those who help themselves' is probably healthier than believing we're puppets on God's string."[3] What we believe about God not only affects our health but our attitudes as well. An attitude of trust drives out fear because fear is basically the denial of trust.

Jim is a retired marketing genius who worked successfully for many years as a consultant with several of Furtune 500 Companies. He and his wife now reside comfortably near Lake Barkley in Kentucky. Recently, he had quadruple by-pass surgery. I asked him how he dealt with that experience. He said, "You know, I've never been the worrying type. I believe in committing your way unto the Lord and trusting Him to take care of you." Lech Walesa, Nobel Prize winner for the Solidarity movement in Poland, once said that deep faith eliminates fear.

However, like the rich fool, there is a tendency in all of us to scheme and plan in order to prepare ourselves for every imaginable and unimaginable problem that may come our way. Disguised as ambition, fear throttles us forward in a fruitless effort to make our future secure. It is interesting to me that, on the heels of the parable of the rich fool, words of Jesus about fear and anxiety come. "Therefore I say to you, do not worry about your life, what you will eat; nor about your body, what you will put on" (Luke 12:22). Luke places these words of Jesus right after this parable while Matthew locates them in the Sermon on the Mount. It seems to me that Luke knows us well. Freedom in life stems not from financial security but from faith in God.

The Priority Analysis

Subject yourself to a frequent priority check. That is the final admonition Jesus makes for managing fear and anxiety. In the last analysis, fear results in the refusal to keep life in its proper perspective. Humans were created by God to live for God. When we live for ourselves, we frustrate God's order of things, and when we do that, it should not surprise us to find anxiety strangling us. "Seek first the kingdom of God" (v. 33) said Jesus. Few commands of Christ could be more explicit. When you feel anxiety pressing against you and fear threatening to overwhelm you, pause long enough to ask yourself: Why am I afraid? Whom or what do I fear? Why am I feeling anxious? To whom or to what cause have I been giving myself lately? What does this tell me about the priorities of my life?

A tragic story appeared in the news one day. An accomplished skydiver and instructor completed a course of instruction for several students who were training to skydive. When the classwork was completed, the instructor and his students strapped on their parachutes, and a plane took them to an altitude of 10,000 feet. It was a beautiful blue-sky day. Visibility was unlimited. The instructor was so proud of his students and their progress toward becoming accomplished skydivers that he decided to take along his videocamera to record the free fall of his associates. The instructor jumped first to record their first attempts at skydiving. One by one they jumped while the camera captured the momentous occasion on videotape. After several seconds of free falling and video recording, the instructor reached for his own rip cord which would trigger the release of his parachute. To his fatal surprise, however, he discovered that, in his excitement over the progress and preparations of his students, he had failed to adequately prepare himself. He had left his own parachute in the classroom. He plunged to his death.

I have thought many times of the need for adequate self-analysis and preparation. While it is true few will face a fate similar to that of the skydiver, many will find their lives coming to a crashing defeat through an unnerving fear or a destructive anxiety. The only safeguard I know is to reorder our priorities. Then, and only then, will we be prepared for our free-falling flight through life.

12
Through Security

Our Guarantee Against the Grim Reaper

(2 CORINTHIANS 5:1-10)

There is a Reaper whose name is Death,
and, with his sickle keen
He reaps the bearded grain at a breath,
And the flowers that grow between.
—H. W. Longfellow

In this descriptive poem, Longfellow captured not only the fate common to all human, animal, and plant life but the fear experienced by all humans in the face of the Grim Reaper. Death is perhaps the only thing all of the human family shares alike. If there's anything we long for, it is a sense of security and confidence against that which appears to be an exit into nothingness. Over the years, I have come to believe that even the most agnostic and atheistic of persons have a longing for security, hope, and God.

When I was a student in seminary, Fred Craddock delivered the Mullins Lectures in Preaching. I heard him tell of the time he was in college in a small mountain school in eastern Tennessee. Before graduating students were required to take a course in "Apologetics" and learn how to defend the Christian faith against agnosticism and atheism. Since there were few identifiable agnostics in the area, Craddock went to the school library to find one. He picked up a copy of the book *The Speeches of Robert Ingersoll of Peoria, Illinois*. Ingersoll was an agnostic and orator of the first order who made a living making fun of Christians. While on a western swing across America, Ingersoll received a telegram that his brother in Washington, D.C., had died. Ingersoll was requested to make a few remarks at the funeral service.

Among those who attended were senators, governors, representatives, and other high officials. A mountain of flowers encircled a flag-draped casket. At the appointed time, Robert Ingersoll, known to some as an agnostic and to others as an atheist, stood to his feet. He gave the eulogy and concluded by saying,

> Life is a narrow vale between the cold
>   barren peaks of two eternities.
> We don't know whence we come,
>   or wither we go.
> We try in vain to see beyond the heights.
> We cry aloud and we hear nothing,
>   but the echo of our own discordant cry.

And then, those who were there said, Ingersoll stopped, looked at the casket, swallowed hard, and ended,

> But in the night of death,
>   hope sees a star,
> And love hears the rustle of a wing.

Craddock perceptively asked, "What did Ingersoll mean by that?"[1] We will probably never know for sure, but it appears that Ingersoll might have been shelving his agnosticism to embrace faith and hope. While we may never know about Ingersoll, I doubt you will ever meet anyone who does not have this longing to know and desire to believe that death does not write the final line on the script of life.

I believe you can have confidence in the presence of the Grim Reaper and hope in the face of death. To the Corinthians, the apostle Paul shared his secret of confidence about death. By listening to his words to them, we can discern the secret for ourselves and raise our own level of confidence.

Facing Your Concerns

One of the first things you notice when reading the apostle Paul's words is how forthrightly he discussed the subject of death. A few years ago, psychologists described our society as a "death-denying" culture. The subject was seldom discussed. People largely pretended it did not exist. In recent years, however, there has developed a morbid preoccupation with death. Browse through a video store and you'll see what I mean. Some of the most popular box-office hits are movies which all but glamorize death. It is unmistakably obvious that there is an increasing interest in the reality of death. Elizabeth Kubler-Ross' book *Life After Life* has become a best-seller. People are fascinated by these documented "out-of-body" experiences some have had. Educators tell us that college courses on "death and dying" are among the most popular with students.

In all of our interest in the subject of death however, there is a curious paradox. We still find it difficult, for the most part, to discuss the subject personally and with any degree of seriousness. It is as if we would prefer to leave the subject to the screenwriters, novelists, and psychologists so as to keep the subject at a safe distance.

In his commentary on *1 and 2 Corinthians*, Ken Chafin tells of a time when, as a college student, he went to work as a salesman for a company that was developing one of the first modern cemeteries in Albuquerque, New Mexico. Chafin was trained for the position and an important part of his training centered on how to handle the objections people might raise to the subject of making their funeral arrangements. One suggestion that stood out in Chafin's memory was this: "If they say that they need some time to discuss it, just ask them how long it's been since they had a serious talk in the family about death. Their answer to that question will prove that although death is one of the inescapable realities of our existence, most people never discuss it."[2]

It's true, isn't it? When was the last time you seriously discussed the subject with a friend or family member? The fact that we so seldom talk about it exposes our anxiety. And, one of the things we can do to overcome our feelings of fear about death is to face our concerns more openly and honestly. The apostle Paul did, and as a result, we are the fortunate recipients of his candidness. Sometimes, I think it might also help us to understand that even Jesus experienced anxiety and fear regarding His own approaching death (Mark

14:33). The fact that He faced it so honestly may have been one of the factors which enabled Him to submit to it with such dignity (Luke 22:42).

Framing Your Convictions

Honestly facing the reality of death, however, is not enough. There is something else we must do to raise our level of confidence in the face of the Grim Reaper. I think it would help each of us to think through our own faith convictions about life, death, and eternity.

What do you believe about life? death? the hereafter? You could ask these questions of the general public and receive as many different responses as there are varieties of ice cream flavors. The views of many people seem fashioned more by what is socially fashionable than by what is validated by Scripture and Christian history. For example, today there are a couple of popular misconceptions about death and the hereafter which are embraced by many people. One is an old idea which has been cloaked in the garment of the New Age philosophy. Reincarnation is really the old Hindu idea of the recycling of the soul. One reaches higher and higher levels of fulfillment as the soul migrates upward through plant and animal life and stages of human life.

The other popular misconception about death and the hereafter is thoroughly materialistic. All life is matter. Therefore, death is the cessation of life. Like a huge "Exit" sign hanging over life, death is an exit into nothingness. There is no afterlife. This life is all there is, so the prevailing philosophy is "Grab all the gusto you can" because, after all, "you only go around once." If the first misconception is based on a circular view of life, this second one is based on a linear view.

Neither view, however, is true. I believe it is important to affirm the view of Scripture. "How do you know the scriptural view is right?" someone might ask. I accept it by faith. Paul said, "For we walk by faith, and not by sight" (v. 7). The truth is, we all walk by faith. I can no more verifiably prove the scriptural view of death and eternity is right than anyone else can disprove it.

Once, I heard a Christian apoligist say he was approached by an atheist who challenged him by saying, "I don't believe in heaven or hell!"

"Well," responded the Christian, "I do. If you're right and I am wrong, then neither of us loses anything. If, however, I am right and you are wrong, you lose everything!"

I wish the apologist would have been more compassionate and less competitive with the disbeliever, but the truth is it takes no more faith to believe what the Bible teaches than it takes to disbelieve it. In fact, the weight of evidence lies on the side of the believer. For centuries, the teachings of Scripture have equipped people for the living of life and encouraged people in the face of death. Since history is replete with countless examples of those who have accepted Scripture and heroically faced death, then the burden of proof lies with the skeptic who chooses to disbelieve.

So, what does the Bible teach? What faith convictions may we frame and hang on the wall of our lives which will enable us to face the reality of death more confidently? The apostle Paul affirms three convictions.

Life Beyond Death

There is really a life beyond death (vv. 1-5). You cannot read this passage without coming away with the distinct impression that either Paul was grossly deceiving his readers or he was gloriously decided about the future which awaited him. Notice how frequently he says, "We know . . ." (vv. 1,6, and 8). In these verses, Paul employs two metaphors about life and death. One is the "earthly tent" and "eternal building." He writes, "For we know that if our earthly house, this tent, is destroyed, we have a building from God, a house not made with hands, eternal in the heavens" (v. 1). Paul is sharply contrasting the temporariness of life, on the one hand, with the permanentness of eternity on the other. Life is fragile as the victims of the 1989 earthquake in Oakland, California, could persuasively testify. Life beyond, however, is permanent and eternal.

The other metaphor is "clothed" and "unclothed." Paul says, "For in this we groan, earnestly desiring to be clothed with our habitation which is from heaven, . . . not because we want to be un-clothed, but further clothed, that mortality may be swallowed up by life" (vv. 2,4). Paul refers to the body as clothing. To the Jewish mind, it was unthinkable to consider ever being without a body: ". . . we shall not be found naked" (v. 3). The promise of Scripture is that we will always be clothed, if not with an earthly body, then with a heavenly, or spiritual, body.

Absent From the Body

To be absent from the body is to be present with the Lord (vv. 6-8). This is the second faith conviction Paul affirms. Recently, a church member asked me, "What happens to us when we die?" There are several interpretations of Scripture at this point. Some say that when we die we enter into a state of sleep and remain in that state until the resurrection at the end of the world (1 Thess. 4:13f). Others say we are disembodied spirits either in Paradise with Jesus or in Hades with the wicked where we await the final judgment when the righteous are awarded with eternal life and wicked eternal damnation. Those who hold this view point to the parable of Laza-rus and Dives in Luke 16:19-31. Still others say that in death one enters a state of timelessness. Therefore, to talk about the resurrec-tion, judgment, or final destination of people and in what sequence these events transpire is fruitless. Timelessness makes it impossible to pinpoint these events precisely.

The truth is none of us knows for sure. One thing is certain, however. At the moment of death, believers are immediately in the presence of Christ. Jesus told the dying thief, "Today you will be with Me in Paradise" (Luke 23:43). That's enough information for any believing person.

Judgment

The third conviction Paul affirms is that, for the conscientious Christian, judgment is not something to dread (vv. 9-10). Judgment is unquestionable to Paul. It need not be something Christians fear because, the truth is, when we ask God's forgiveness, all of life's failures recorded on the videotape of our lives is spliced out and destroyed. For the Christian, judgment will be based not on the question of salvation or the quantity of service but rather on the quality of one's service for Christ.

The missionary, musician, and surgeon, Albert Schweitzer, who turned his back on a lucrative career to go to Africa as a medical missionary, was once asked by a reporter, "Dr. Schweitzer, have you found happiness in Africa?"

He replied, "I have found a place of service and that is enough happiness for anyone."

Embracing these solid faith convictions will enable you to face death more confidently.

Finding Your Confidence

The most startling yet helpful suggestion apostle Paul makes to the Corinthians is the one recorded in verse 5. "Now He who has prepared us for this very thing is God, who also has given us the Spirit as a guarantee." Confidence in the face of death is a gift which God gives us by virtue of the indwelling Spirit of Christ. The source of freedom from the fear of death is none other than the Spirit Himself. When a person becomes a believer, the Spirit is "deposited" by God in his or her heart as a "first installment" of what is to come. It is a "down payment" God makes to us with the promise that more is forthcoming. The promise of Jesus given to His followers was, "And if I go and prepare a place for you, I will come again and receive you to Myself; that where I am, there you may be also" (John 14:3). Christ guaranteed us that there is life beyond this life, and we acknowledge and accept it confidently in the very depth of our being. He confirms this truth in our hearts by His Spirit. The point is that, ultimately, our confidence in the face of death is a gift God gives us. Coming to terms with our mortality, therefore, is a process which the Holy Spirit begins the moment He takes up residence in our lives by faith.

Recently, I received a letter from an institution informing me that a check for $1,500 was enclosed. I was happily surprised but also suspicious. It read: "'Preferred Customer' we would like you to cash the enclosed check and spend it on whatever you wish—a new car, a vacation to the Bahamas, or a new bedroom suite for your wife."

After looking more closely, however, I discovered it was a savings and loan institution, and they were willing to loan us the money, although we had not applied for it, because of our excellent credit rating. I later learned that anybody with good credit is likely to be designated a "Preferred Customer" and receive a similar check by mail. Perhaps you have received such a letter yourself.

The whole episode reminded me that, in many ways, God is like a "Preferred Customer" whose credit rating is impeccable. He can be trusted to follow through on His promise of eternal life. The Holy Spirit is God's "first installment" of eternal life, and when we accept His divine down payment, one of the gifts we receive is confidence that He will keep His promise. Accept His gift of confidence. It's yours for the receiving.

For the Christian, coming to terms with mortality involves facing your concerns about death, framing your convictions about life and eternity, and supremely, receiving God's gift of confidence—the Holy Spirit. If you will, the Grim Reaper will not be such a grim reality.

13
Through Perseverance
The Christian's Olympiad
(HEBREWS 12:1-2)

"It matters not whether you win or lose, but how you run the race." Those words were engraved on a plaque which hung on my bedroom wall, when I was a child. Today, however, the motto would probably read differently. "It matters whether you win or lose, no matter how you run the race." Few things seem more important these days than winning. Vince Lombardi once captured in a statement the prevailing philosophy of our times. "Winning isn't everything," he observed, "it's the only thing!" The desire to win at all costs has precipitated a ends-means inversion. Athletes and athletic departments have fallen victim to the temptation to use any means to achieve the winning edge over the competition. Sometimes, the "means" takes the shape of steroids. At other times, it's money given and special privileges promised to young recruits in an effort to entice them to sign a contract. Even as I write this chapter, a major university in the state in which I live is under investigation by the NCAA for allegations of improper recruiting practices.

Is winning everything? It depends upon how you define a winner. Is the winner the person or team who walks away with the trophy? Or is the real winner the competitor who can say at the end of the race, "I ran the race to the best of my ability." I believe it is the latter. And, in our better moments, I think we all know that winning has more to do with the character and conduct of the competitor than with the conclusion to the competition.

During the Winter Olympics in 1988, speed skater Dan Jansen fell twice on the ice to the dismay of all spectators. Some believe his difficulty was due to the fact that his sister died unexpectedly prior to the games. Sports analysts wrote about how disappointing it was that Jansen lost, but I know better. To me, Jansen was not a loser at all. Granted, he did not walk away with the gold. But, I'm certain he left with the satisfaction of knowing, under difficult circumstances, he had done the best he could.

In the final analysis, it is true that what really matters is not whether you win or lose, but how you run the race. What's true of the athletic world is true of the spiritual world as well. God is not looking for people with bulging trophy cases, but for people who are willing to do their very best with what opportunities and gifts they have. Look at the eleventh chapter of the Book of Hebrews. Someone has called it "God's Hall of Fame." But, if you look closely, the persons listed there are hardly extraordinary by any standard. One is Abraham who, at seventy-five years of age, decided to leave his homeland on a journey to who knows where. Can you imagine what his neighbors thought? Then there's Jacob, a man whose life was characterized by deceit. There's Joseph who was despised and rejected by his brothers and yet became secretary of state over Egypt. There's Moses whose level of self-confidence would qualify him for a course of study with Dale Carnegie. There's Rahab the harlot whose name alone would be frowned upon. There's Gideon, Samson, David, and. . . . I hope you get the point. God is not looking for outstanding people, but people who are willing to stand out from the normal flow of the crowd and deposit their best efforts and gifts at His disposal.

Run the race of your life to the best of your ability. God asks for no more, but He expects no less. "Therefore we also," says the writer of Hebrews in the first verse of chapter 12. Here the writer links us to the list of persons in God's Hall of Fame. Why? Because the writer wants to motivate us to desire to be listed among those whom God calls the real winners in the race of life. You can be a real winner. You can run the race set before you and run it well. However, there are several things you must know. The writer of Hebrews describes what you must know and do to be listed among those in God's Hall of Fame.

Never Alone

In the race for the meaning of life itself, it is important to know that none of us is left alone, but we are surrounded by spectators and sympathetic supporters. "Since we are surrounded by so great a cloud of witnesses," says the writer of Hebrews. Picture yourself poised on the starting line of a running track and stadium filled with loyal, supportive fans, and you've caught something of the metaphor used by the writer to describe our experience.

None of us runs the race of life in isolation. God has no Lone Rangers. At times, you may feel alone. Like Elijah, you may feel as if you are the only one who has stayed with the race and refused to toss in the towel. I'm sure there are times when all of us feel like the little boy who was asked by his mother to do something he was not inclined to do. Late one evening, she was cleaning the kitchen and asked her son to go to the back porch and fetch the broom. Knowing it was dark and scary on the back porch, he panicked.

"But, Mommy," he argued, "it's dark out there and you know how I'm scared of the dark!"

"Nonsense," she replied. Seeing this as an opportunity to teach her son a lesson on the omnipresence of God, she instructed, "Son, don't you know God is everywhere? Now, march out there right now and fetch the broom!"

Walking reluctantly to the door, he cracked it just enough to peer into the darkness, and said timidly, "Say, Lord, if you're out there, would you mind handing me the broom?"

What the young lad was feeling, I have felt. And, so have you. The writer, however, wants us to know the same thing the mother wanted her son to know. We are never anywhere that God isn't there beside us. God is like an encouraging coach who gives instructions, offers advice, and, more than anything else, simply reminds us by His presence that we are not alone in the race.

In addition to God's presence, there is a stadium filled with our fans. Who are these that make up the "great . . . cloud of witnesses?" The writer is not explicit. I think he is referring to all God's saints who have finished life's race and now fill the grandstands to encourage the rest of us. Have you ever had the feeling that a loved one or some beloved Christian saint who had gone on to be with the Lord was still with you at times? Perhaps it was during a crisis or a personal difficulty but, unassumingly and unexpectedly, a sense of calmness and peace passed over you as that saint's presence is felt by you. Who knows but that the spirit of that person is really with you? If it is true that "to be absent from the body [is] to be present with the Lord" (2 Cor. 5:8) and the Lord, by His spirit, is with us at all times, then why should it be hard to believe that the spirits of God's saints surround us from the stadium of the earth's atmosphere?

I believe, as you run the race of life God has set before you and look with the eyes of faith toward the grandstands, you will see all of God's saints waving their arms wildly in your support. If you will, you'll find yourself running your race more effectively, efficiently, and energetically.

Scrapping Unnecessary Weight

Scrap unnecessary weight. We must do this, if the race is to be run well. Don't carry around excess baggage. "Let us lay aside every weight," counsels the writer of Hebrews, "and the sin which so easily ensnares us." Every good runner knows that to run well you must divest yourself of unnecessary weight. Imagine how ridiculous it would appear to see a runner in a three piece suit wearing a pair of tennis shoes. Every serious runner strips down to his T-shirt and running shorts and shoes. The writer has taken this reality and applied it to the Christian life. In the race of life, every Christian, if he or she is to run well, must cast off the weights which will hinder progress or make the race more difficult.

What are the weights which hinder us? They are the sins "which clings so closely" (RSV). This phrase could be translated in two different ways, both of which have meaning to us. On the one hand, it could be translated, "every clinging sin." On the other hand, however, it might be rendered, "every sin to which we cling." Some sins cling to us while some of us cling to sin. Either way, sin ensnares us.

What are the sins to which you cling or that cling to you which need stripping off? Again, the writer is not explicit. However, I do believe there are some sins which every Christian needs to scrap.

First, scrap negativism. Few things hinder Christians more than a critical, negative spirit. I heard about a man who approached the new pastor of his church and said, "Reverend, I want you to know I don't like much of what goes on around here, and I'll always be sure to let you know about it!"

"But why would you want to be so critical?" asked the perplexed minister.

"Because," explained the man, "that's the one and only talent I have!"

"If that's the case," retorted the pastor, "then I have but one suggestion to make to you. Remember in the parable of the talents, one man who went out and buried his talent in the ground?"

"Yes," replied the man.

"Go thou," admonished the pastor, "and do likewise!"

Second, scrap the spirit of unforgiveness. Most Christians seem blind to the halting effects unforgiveness bears on their own progress in the race.

The founder of modern theology, Immanuel Kant, hired a man whose name was Lampe to keep his books. One day Kant discovered Lampe had been juggling the books and stealing from him. When he confronted Lampe about it, Kant said, "I have chosen not to prosecute you, but to forgive you." That night, and every night thereafter, Kant wrote in his diary just before retiring to bed, "Don't forget to forgive Lampe!"

Forgiveness is a choice we make. I often hear people say, "But I can't forgive!" Sure, we can. It would be more honest to say, "I refuse to forgive." The cripples in life's race are always those who withhold forgiveness.

And, then, scrap apathy and indifference. We live in a world where few seem to care about anything. A television documentary concerning the ecological crisis facing our world was shown recently. The former CBS news commentator, Walter Cronkite, was narrating the program. Cronkite said, "In a recent survey, public apathy was identified as the most serious culprit in the ecological crisis faced by our nation." In short, he was saying that people just don't seem to care anymore. Unfortunately, this attitude is even found among Christians. It is little wonder the church runs poorly in the race God has set before her. The typical church today has far too many team members who seem content to sit on the bench and avoid involvement in the race. It is not that they don't have any interest in the game. They simply refuse to become involved. They remind me of the little creatures in the children's story of the Little Red Hen.

One day a hen found a grain of wheat and said to her friends, "Who'll help me plant the wheat?"

"Not I," said the duck.

"Not I," said the cat.

"Not I," said the pig.

"All right," said the Little Red Hen. "I'll do it myself." And so, she did.

When the wheat had grown into a plant, she asked, "Who'll help me cut the wheat, grind it into flour, and bake a loaf of bread?"

"Not I," said the three, respectively.

When the loaf of bread had been baked, she asked, "Who'll help me eat the bread?

"I will," said the duck.

"I will," said the cat.

"I will," said the pig.

"Oh no, you won't," remarked the Little Red Hen. "You did not help me plant, cut, thresh, or carry the wheat to the mill. Nor did you help me bake the bread. So, you won't help me eat it, either. I'll eat it all by myself." And so, she did.

I'm not suggesting we be stingy like the Little Red Hen. I am suggesting we get involved and refuse to be like the duck, cat, and pig.

Stick-to-It-Ness

To run the race and run it well, don't give up, but keep striving onward. "Let us run with patience" (KJV) says the writer of Hebrews. *Patience* translates from a Greek word meaning *endurance.* The best paraphrase of the word might be "stick-to-it-ness." Everyone runs the race at a different pace. Some grow quickly in the Christian faith. Others grow slowly. The important thing is that we keep growing and going, even when it gets tough.

A recent documentary, *Destined to Live* was a report about how several women in our society, some of whom are well-known actresses, have handled the shattering news that they have cancer. One woman, who was recovering from cancer surgery, said, "My philosophy now is that, when life kicks you, you should let it kick you forward." I like that philosophy. God has not promised that our race will be easy. He has promised, however, when our race is finished, there is a reward awaiting those who have stayed with the race and have refused to give up.

Watching people over the years as they have struggled to remain faithful in spite of unbelievable odds, I've come to believe there are two things to remember which, if followed, will always keep you in the race. The first is, when life gets tough, don't forget that God can use your difficulties to make you a better person. It is not that God is the author of trouble, but God is the architect who, through trouble, can design a new you.

Once I heard an articulate minister from Dallas, Frederick Haynes, tell of an imaginary conversation he had one morning with a tea bag. As he dropped the tea bag in and out of the cup of hot water, the tea bag spoke out, "Frederick, do you know what tea bags and Christians have in common?"

"No," he responded, perplexed.

"Neither of us," explained the tea bag, "is of much use until we've passed through some hot water."

It makes sense, doesn't it? Our usefulness in life is somehow strangely attached to our struggles through life. Calvin Miller once wrote, "Most of those who care about the fallen have known the pain of falling!"[1]

There's a second thing to remember which will keep you in the race when life gets tough. Keep life's nobler purposes in perspective. When life presses upon you, the temptation is to see only the immediate and to forget the ultimate. Some people are farsighted. They see things at a distance better than those objects close up. Others are nearsighted. They see things up close but have difficulty seeing those things which are at a distance. Under the duress of difficulty, people are usually nearsighted. They see all too well the problems at hand but, unfortunately, lose sight of the possibilities which lie just beyond them. Keeping life's nobler purposes in perspective will help you, when life gets tough, to maintain a farsightedness. The problems before you will be held in check by the grander purposes beyond you.

In short, knowing "why" you're in the race will keep you in the race. Richard Bach, author of *Jonathan Livingston Seagull*, once wrote, "Here's a test to find whether your mission on earth is finished: If you're alive, it isn't."[2] Keeping life's mission in mind will always keep your problems in line.

Never Looking Back

Keep your eyes fixed on Jesus and never look back. That's the final suggestion the author makes to help us run our race well. "Looking unto Jesus," says the writer, "the author and finisher of our faith." In track and field, if a runner is to win the race, he or she must keep his or her eyes firmly fixed on the finish line. If not, the race may be lost. So, keep going. Don't get sidetracked or distracted. Keep looking unto Jesus who stands at the end of life's race waiting to crown you with victory and honor.

In William Johnson's commentary on Hebrews, there is the true story of the times when two great milers met in the British Empire Games in Vancouver, British Columbia, on August 7, 1954. In what was hailed as the famous "Miracle Mile," two of the world's fastest runners met to compete. The first was Roger Bannister, a twenty-five-year-old medical student who had previously shattered the world record by running a mile in under four minutes. The second was John Landy, a twenty-four-year-old Australian who was the second man in recorded history to crack the four-minute mile. And now, in Vancouver, these two runners were competing before a crowd of 35,000 people.

Bannister let Landy set the pace throughout most of the race. Sports analysts commented on the athletic shrewdness of Bannister because, while Landy knew he had the lead, he did not know the extent of his lead. Curiosity got the best of him. During the last 100 yards of the race, Landy turned his head, momentarily, to look back. Then Bannister, with a tremendous burst of speed, passed him to win the race by just five yards.[3]

Get the point? So, stay in the race. Keep your eyes glued upon Christ who is the author and finisher of your race. And remember, while it is true, "It matters not whether you win or lose, but how you run the race." If you will follow the rules of the race set forth by the writer of Hebrews, you'll not only run the race well, but you'll be a real winner in the best sense of the word.

14
Through Devotion
Running on Empty

(PSALM 46:10; LUKE 10:38 TO 11:13)

Early one Sunday morning, my son and I ran out of gas on the way to church. Wondering what should we do, I thought of all the things I wanted to say to my wife, none of which were very pastoral, for driving the car the week before and letting the fuel tank get so low. But then, I remembered that I was the one who had driven the car the week before. She had driven the other car. So, I scolded myself for not having the fuel gauge fixed by the dealer when we first bought the car. The fuel gauge has never worked right. You can fill up the tank and the gauge will register full. But, once it gets down to half a tank, the gauge drops to "E," and it's a guessing game thereafter.

Since we were only a block away from our house, I said, "Jonathan, let's walk back to the house and get a can of gas." We did. Within minutes, we were back only to discover there was no funnel through which to pour the gas into the tank. I knew then it was not going to be a good day. I mumbled a few things under my breath.

Pouring the gasoline from the can, I managed to get enough into the tank to start the car. However, most of it splashed on the ground, and my shoes, and my pants legs. I went to church that day about half mad, smelling like a service station attendant who had just gotten off duty.

After that experience which, parenthetically, has happened more than once, I have thought how similar the experience is to the maintenance of our spiritual lives. Most of us attempt to run on empty most of the time. Our spiritual lives are like an automobile that must have fuel in which to operate. However, all too frequently, we either ignore the fuel gauge of our lives which signals our need for spiritual fuel or the gauge of our lives works so inadequately that we are unaware of our spiritual needs until our lives come to a surprising halt. In either case, the result is the same—emptiness, frustration, and failure.

Fuel is to an automobile as your devotional life is to the maintenance of your spiritual life. Without the energy which comes from prayer, meditation, and the study of the Bible, your "spiritual-mobile" simply will not go. But, then, we know that, right? So, what's the problem? Why is it difficult for us to translate what we know into what we do? If you're like me, I have struggled most of my Christian life to develop a consistent, habitual devotional life. On New Year's Eve, every year, I resolved to find more time to pray, meditate, and read the Bible. While I usually started out well, it was not long before I was back in an all too familiar pattern of striving to keep my spiritual engine running. Because of this, I have spent most of my early Christian pilgrimage burdened by guilt and the feeling that my Christian life was a failure.

Over the years, I have learned a few of those forces, against which we wrestle, make the development of consistent and meaningful devotional life difficult. In the paragraphs that follow, I will identify a few of them.

The "Busy" Life

"Beware of the barrenness of busy life." Those words appeared as a motto on the desk of Fred Mitchell, a leader in missions.[1]

Henri Nouwen, in *The Way of the Heart* writes:

> In general we are very busy people. We have many meetings to attend, many visits to make, many services to lead. Our calendars are filled with appointments, our days and weeks filled with engagements, and our years filled with plans and projects. There is seldom a period in which we do not know what to do, and we move through life in such a distracted way that we do not even take the time and rest to wonder if any of the things we think, say or do are worth thinking, saying, or doing. We simply go along with the many "musts" and

"oughts" that have been handed to us, and we live with them as if they were authentic translations of the Gospel of our Lord.[2]

From my earliest days, I was taught to stay busy doing something. I was promised it would produce two worthwhile dividends. One, it would keep me out of trouble. And, two, it would make me more productive. Well, keeping busy did keep me from getting into trouble, at least some of the time. But, staying busy did not always make me more productive. In fact, the opposite seemed to be the case. The busier I became the less productive I was. Being the high-energy person I innately am, I could oversee a marathon of activities. However, instead of feeling fulfilled and accomplished, I often felt frustrated and empty. Someone has aptly described our age as a "gassed-up, geared-up, on-the-go society." But, somewhere along the way, we have forgotten, or never learned, that where we're headed so hurriedly may not be where we really want to go.

Out in front of our suite of church offices is a stop sign and a dip in the street. The sign reads "Stop Dip." The sign has become a symbol of a need in my own life. I sometimes say to myself with a little humor but a lot of seriousness, "Stop Dip! Try slowing down a bit. You can't do it all. Take care of yourself. Pray more often. And, don't forget there is nothing more barren than a busy life." You see, one of the forces against which we struggle to develop a devotional life is the powerful myth that we must be very busy, activity-oriented people if we are to be productive people. Until we can stop trying, without feeling guilty, to do everything we think must be done, we will have a hard time shaking the shame we feel for neglecting our spiritual lives. The psalmist said, "Be still, and know that I am God" (Ps. 46:10). Until we can learn to do that, a consistent and rewarding devotional life will escape us.

Your View of God

Our view of God often gets in our way, too. Some people think of God as a Scrooge-like tyrant from whom little, if anything, can be squeezed. Others think of God like children think of Santa Claus—a person from whom anything, if not everything, can be taken.

Against these two erroneous views, Jesus gave us a view of God that is like neither of these extremes.

Once, Jesus told the story about a man who came to the house of his friend at midnight. The lights were out. The door was shut. The friend and his family were in bed asleep. But, around midnight, the neighbor pounded on his door pleading for help.

"What do you want?" asked the friend from inside the house.

"Do you have any bread you could spare? cried the neighbor. "A friend, I've not seen in ages, dropped by unexpectedly, and I have nothing to set before him!"

"Go away!" shouted the man. "It's late, and we're in bed."

You would suspect at this point the neighbor would have taken the suggestion and proceeded to another home or a convenience store nearby. Instead, however, he proceeded to slap his hands against the friend's door until he was forced to get up and supply his need.

The whole story is rather humorous. Yet, Jesus is serious in what He's telling us about the nature of God. He is not telling us that God is like a friend who must be coerced into responding to an obvious need. Jesus is using what Lloyd Ogilvie calls a "more than that" method of teaching. It's like He is saying, "If a friend will finally respond because of the harassment of a neighbor, how much more quickly will God respond to our needs."[3]

The neighbor came at midnight. The door was shut. The sign on the door read, "Do Not Disturb." With God, however, it's different. We may come to Him at any hour, day or night. His door is always open. The sign on His door reads, "Come to Me, all you who labor and are heavy laden, and I will give you rest" (Matt. 11:28).

When we view God as a reluctant neighbor from whom we must plead for everything and convince of anything, it will be hard to look upon Him favorably, even harder to know Him intimately. The truth is, you will not want to know Him.

Seeing God, on the other hand, as a friend who door is already open and whose readiness to respond is greater than our willingness to ask makes intimacy not only possible but desirable. Such a view of God will actually fuel your spiritual engine and throttle you toward God.

If some view God as a stingy tyrant, others view Him as a heavenly Santa Claus. This opposite extreme is equally as damaging to the maintenance of a devotional life. To correct this misconception of God, Jesus asked what a father might do if his son were to ask him for bread. "Give him a stone instead? What if he should ask for a fish, would he give him a serpent instead.

"Of course not," we respond, just as Jesus hearers must have responded. Then comes Jesus' punchline. "If you then, being evil, know how to give good gifts to your children, how much more will your heavenly Father give the Holy Spirit to those who ask Him!" (v. 13).

If your view of God is that of a cosmic Santa Claus who will give you anything you ask, what happens to your relationship to Him when that for which you ask is withheld? It seems to me you are left with no alternative but to conclude, either you have been a bad boy or girl and no longer deserving of His gifts, or God is someone other than you thought Him to be. In either case, He becomes to you a God who gives stones instead of bread, serpents instead of fish. And, who wants to know that kind of God?

Do you see what this view of God does to your relationship to Him. Ultimately, it distances you from Him. That's why, in Luke's version of these words of Jesus, there is a qualifier, ". . . how much more will your heavenly Father give the Holy Spirit to those who ask Him!" (v. 13). What does God give us when we pray to Him? He gives us Himself. He doesn't give us "things." As long as we seek "things" from God, then God is little more than an object we use. When, however, we seek God Himself, then God is a subject with whom we may relate, intimately and personally.

A Discipline Learned and a Learned Discipline

From a practical standpoint, the devotional life is a discipline that is learned. In fact, it is both a discipline that is learned and a learned discipline. Let me explain. One day, when Jesus ceased praying, a disciple said to Him, "Lord, teach us to pray" (v. 1). Jesus gave him what we know as the Model Prayer. Why? Because there is a right way and a wrong way to pray. The devotional life, therefore, is a discipline that is learned. For example, if you study carefully the Lord's Prayer, you will discover it contains many different dimensions of prayer. There is adoration and praise, confession and submission, intercession and petition, and gratitude and thanksgiving.

Think for a moment about your own prayer life. Does it contain the variety you find in the Lord's Prayer? Is it balanced? If your prayers are like mine, they tend to be a little lopsided. I have no trouble petitioning God for those things I perceive as needs. I have to remind myself, however, to pray for others, express gratitude, and, very often, simply adore and praise God without bringing my checklist of wants and wishes to Him.

There is much to learn about all of the dimensions of the devotional life. Take the Bible, for example. The reason we have a hard time reading the Bible is because few of us ever learn how to read the Bible. Bible reading is a laborious exercise if you read it like you do the morning paper. If, however, the Bible is read like one would read a personal letter from a friend or a novel whose central character is you, the reader, then it takes on a life of its own and becomes an enriching experience.

What about silence and solitude? I think, perhaps, this is the hardest discipline of the devotional life to learn. We know so little about silence because we've become so accustomed to noise. Yet, the longer I live, the more convinced I become that the most rewarding aspect of a devotional life is learning how to be still and listen to the silence. The value of learning how to enter into silence is that, when we emerge from solitude, we hear more clearly. E. Glenn Hinson once wrote:

> Silence can sensitize. Silence, of course, requires solitude. Solitude is what sent thousands of the best and the brightest youth scurrying to the desert to find God during the fourth and fifth centuries. Today only a few will choose this as a way of life. But all who seek wholeness

will require some kind of solitude where, in silence, they can listen to "the still, small voice."[4]

You will spend a greater part of your life seeking to learn all there is to know and experience in prayer, meditation, Scripture study, and solitude. But, for every serious seeker after a devotional life, it is a search worth making and a discipline worth practicing. That is why the devotional life is also a learned discipline. It takes work and effort. I saw an ad recently in the "Wanted" section of a newspaper. It read: "Wanted: To trade an exercise bike for a weigh scale that weighs up to 350 lbs." It's easier, isn't it, to just get a bigger scale than it is to exercise? What exercise is to your body life, the spiritual disciplines are to your spirit life. None of us should ever expect the spiritual engines of our lives to take us very far in our Christian journey without the disciplined and habitual stops necessary for refueling.

The Choice Is Yours

"Destiny is molded more by choice than by chance." Whoever said that is right. Developing a devotional life is a choice we make. It will never happen by accident. Do you remember the time Jesus entered the home of Mary and Martha? (see Luke 10:38-42). Martha was busy with household chores. Mary, however, sat at Jesus' feet, drinking in His words. Ever so often, Martha would peer through the kitchen door resenting the fact that Mary did nothing to help her. Finally, in frustration, Martha stormed into the presence of Mary and Jesus and demanded an explanation as to why she had to serve while Mary simply sat. Jesus reminded Martha that life is a choice and Mary had chosen what was best. Martha had chosen to serve, while Mary had chosen something superior—namely, to sit at Jesus' feet and listen.

Jesus said, "Martha, Martha, you are worried and troubled about many things" (v. 41). What was it that worried and troubled Martha? We're not told, but, I suspect, out of her internal reservoir of "shoulds" and "oughts," she was doing what she felt she ought to do. What she was doing was not bad, however. There is a need to serve. What Martha was doing was right; it was her timing that was wrong. There's a time for serving, but there is also a time for being served. In contrast, Mary's timing was right. She seized the opportunity to be served by Christ. The devotional life is our opportunity to be served and have our spiritual fuel reserves filled. We pray, meditate, and study God's Word not because that's something God wants from us, but something we need from Him. It's the one thing we really need. It is the only thing which cannot be taken from us. Other things may be taken from us—our positions, health, and financial security. The benefits that come to us via the devotional life can never be taken from us.

In many ways, there is a Martha and Mary in all of us. But, most of us are more like Martha than we are Mary. We know how to serve. We race from activity to activity, meeting needs along the way and ministering in the name of Christ. There's always something else that needs to be done or some other person who needs to be seen. It's an endless enterprise that usually ends in restlessness and resentment. Few of us, however, have made friends with the Mary in us. We're just not comfortable sitting. But, such a position is the posture of a devotional life. Make friends with Mary. Let Christ serve you through the medium of your devotional life. If you don't, Mary and Martha will bicker all through your Christian life. And Martha, the part of your personality which drives you to serve, will always win over Mary, the part of your personality which deserves to be served. Using the metaphor of an automobile, Martha is your engine, but Mary is your fuel. Both are needed.

Notes

Chapter 1

1. *USA Weekend,* December 19-21, 1986.

2. "Harvard Psychiatrist Resigns Over Plagarism," *Courier Journal,* November 29, 1988, 1.

3. D. Stuart Briscoe, "Romans" in *The Communicator's Commentary* (Waco: Word Books, 1982), 89.

4. A. M. Hunter, "The Epistle to the Romans," in *The Torch Bible Commentaries* (London: SCM Press LTD, 1957), 46-47.

Chapter 2

1. For a fuller treatment of the subjects of "revolutionary" and "evolutionary" conversion experiences, read John Claypool's book *Glad Reunion* (Waco: Word Books, 1985), 73-79.

2. For a detailed description of "general" and "special" revelation, read Dale Moody's book *The Word of Truth* (Grand Rapids: William B. Eerdmans Publishing Co., 1981), 57-77.

Chapter 3

1. Harold S. Kushner, *When Bad Things Happen to Good People* (New York: Avon Books, 1981), 56.

2. Frederick Buechner, *Wishful Thinking* (New York: Harper & Row Publishers, 1973), 89.

3. Frank Pollard, *Keeping Free* (Nashville: Broadman Press, 1983), 54-55.

Chapter 5

1. Kenneth L. Chafin, sermon "Mission to America," vol. 16, no. 9 (Louisville, Ky.: Walnut St. Baptist Church, March 7, 1985).

2. H. Stephen Shoemaker, *Retelling the Biblical Story* (Nashville: Broadman Press, 1985), 93.

3. *Western Recorder,* February 18, 1986.

4. Elton Trueblood, *The Best of Elton Trueblood,* James R. Newby (Nashville: Impact Books, 1979), 31.

5. Shoemaker, 95.

Chapter 6

1. John N. Gladstone, "A Magnificent Faith" (Hantsport, Nova Scotia: Lancelot Press, 1979), 96.

2. "Hawkings Race Against Time," *Courier Journal,* July 24, 1989.

Chapter 7

1. Kenneth L. Chafin, sermon, "Learning to Enjoy Giving," vol. 16, no. 42 (Louisville, Ky.: Walnut St. Baptist Church, October 31, 1985).

Chapter 9

1. Elton Trueblood, *Your Other Vocation* (New York: Harper & Brothers, 1952), 75.

Chapter 10

1. Elton Trueblood, *The Best of Elton Trueblood,* ed. James R. Newby (Nashville: Impact Books, 1979), 122-23.

Chapter 11

1. "The Big Chill," *Courier Journal,* September 22, 1988, 13.

2. Kenneth L. Chafin, *How to Know When You've Got It Made* (Waco: Word Books, 1981), 123-24.

3. "A Healthy Dose of Religion," *Psychology Today,* November 1988, 14-15.

Chapter 12

1. Fred Craddock told this story in a sermon/lecture he delivered during the Mullins lectures at The Southern Baptist Theological Seminary, Louisville, Kentucky, March 1987.

2. Kenneth Chafin, "1 and 2 Corinthians," *The Communicator's Commentary,* ed. Lloyd Ogilive (Waco; Word Books, 1985), 234.

Chapter 13

1. Calvin Miller, *Becoming: Your Self in the Making* (Old Tappan, N.J.: Fleming H. Revell Co., 1987), 137.

2. Bernie S. Siegel, *Love, Medicine, and Miracles* (New York: Harper & Row, 1986), 83-84.

3. William G. Johnsson, *Hebrews* (Atlanta: John Knox Press, 1980), 86.

Chapter 14

1. Gordon MacDonald, *Ordering Your Private World* (Nashville: Thomas Nelson, Inc., 1984), 17-18.

2. Henri J. M. Nouwen, *The Way of the Heart* (San Francisco: Harper & Row, 1981), 21-22.

3. Lloyd John Ogilvie, *Autobiography of God* (Ventura, Calif.: Regal Books, 1979), 181.

4. E. Glenn Hinson, "A Minister's Devotional Life," *Pulpit Digest* 119:496 (March-April 1989): 72.